7 BOOKS THAT ROCKED THE CHURCH

D A N I E L A . C R A N E

7 BOOKS THAT ROCKED THE CHURCH

HENDRICKSON PUBLISHERS

7 Books That Rocked the Church

© 2018 Daniel A. Crane

Hendrickson Publishers Marketing, LLC
P. O. Box 3473
Peabody, Massachusetts 01961-3473
www.hendrickson.com

ISBN 978-1-68307-194-5

Printed in the United States of America

First Printing—November 2018

Library of Congress Cataloging-in-Publication Data

A catalog record for this title is available from the Library of Congress
Hendrickson Publishers Marketing, LLC ISBN 978-1-68307-194-5

In memory of my grandfather, Clifford Cecil Crane
(May 25, 1919–October 11, 2006)
He made his living on the railroad but came alive with his books

Contents

Acknowledgments ix

Introduction 1

1. Valentinus's *Gospel of Truth*: Who Doesn't Love a Gnostic
   Conspiracy Theory? 7

2. Galileo's *Two Chief World Systems*: A Scandal of Religion,
   Science, and Politics 27

3. Voltaire's *Candide*: Enlightenment Rationalism and the
   Church's Thin Skin 48

4. Charles Darwin's *Origin of Species*: The Many Faces of
   Evolutionary Theory 65

5. Karl Marx's *Communist Manifesto*: The Red Bull
   of the Masses 89

6. Sigmund Freud's Ego and *The Future of an Illusion* 111

7. Joseph Campbell's *Hero with a Thousand Faces*:
   Christianity As an (Almost) Enlightened Myth 133

8. Conclusion: The Next Seven Books 151

Discussion Questions 161

Notes 171

Selected Bibliography 181

Acknowledgments

This book owes much to the support, encouragement, and thoughtful insights of brothers and sisters at Knox Presbyterian Church in Ann Arbor, Michigan, including Pastor Bob Lynn, James Paternoster, and many active participants in a Christian education class on "Books That Rocked the Church." I also received valuable comments and encouragement from Donald Crane, Beatrice Crane, Eric Crane, and Saara Kanervikkoaho-Crane.

Introduction

The church has long had an ambivalent relationship with books. On the one hand, the Christian faith is grounded in a book—*The Book*—so believers respect the written word. Christian authors writing on Christian themes have produced some of the outstanding works of the Western canon, from Saint Augustine's *Confessions*, to John Milton's *Paradise Lost*, to John Bunyan's *Pilgrim's Progress*, to Blaise Pascal's *Pensées*, to pretty much anything by C. S. Lewis.

On the other hand, the church has had a less than cordial relationship with books it found objectionable. One has to look no further than the nineteenth chapter of the book of Acts to witness the emergence of Christian conflict with suspect writings. The apostle Paul had been preaching and performing miracles in the city of Ephesus in Asia Minor (present-day Turkey). Some Jews tried to mimic Paul's exorcisms of evil spirits, and they ended up beaten and naked. The fear of God fell on the Jews and Greeks of the city, leading to a mass burning of sorcery scrolls valued at 50,000 drachmae or about $100,000 today.

This was far from the last time the church would sponsor a book burning. Over its two-thousand-year history, the church has repeatedly had run-ins with dissenting books—works of theology, science, philosophy, political theory, psychology, literature, and social criticism. In some cases, Christians have responded with patient, thoughtful refutation. But, alas, a measured response has not been the norm. More typically, the church has deployed a variety of coercive tactics to suppress the offending work. These tactics have included ad hominem attacks on the author, censorship, destruction, criminalization, threats, condemnation to hell, and overt warfare.

Perhaps most counterproductively, Christians have often asserted absolute irreconcilability between the challenged work and the Christian faith: "If his argument is right, then our faith is wrong." Such assertions can create severe difficulties for the church if the book's argument turns out to be demonstrably correct (as with Galileo's theory of heliocentricism), or eventually believed by a majority of Christians (as with aspects of Darwin's theory of evolution). Even where the church has not been embarrassed by later developments in human understanding, its response to challenging books has often cost it credibility with people who might otherwise have been open to the Christian message. In short, the church's response to books it feared has often created unnecessary obstacles to the church's mission in the world.

SEVEN BOOKS

This book concerns seven seminal books that rocked the Christian church. These works range in date from the second century after Christ to the twentieth century. The authors hailed from various parts of the Western world, from Europe, the Middle East, North Africa, and North America. Their subjects spanned a wide range of topics including the meaning of Christ's life and death, the earth's revolution around the sun, ecclesiastical hypocrisy, evolution through natural selection, social class and economic oppression, the patterns of the human brain, and the commonality of myths. The authors wrote in different styles and for different audiences. Although they surely would not all have agreed with one another, they had this in common: Their works profoundly upset the church by calling into question foundational Christian doctrines or beliefs. Whether because the author meant to do so or because the church found something threatening in the message, each book provoked a sharp response from the church. Most of the books were banned at some time by Christian authorities, and those that could not be banned were subjected to vitriolic condemnation.

These seven books did not offend the church through lewdness or moral depravity. Their offense lay not in their appeal to the libido but to the mind. They did not make libelous charges against Christian icons that required factual correction; they challenged the church by advocating alternative ways to think and consequently to live. In other words, they provided a rival *intellectual* narrative to the biblical story and hence rocked the structure of Christian belief. These were the most dangerous kind of books, and therefore ones that needed the most compelling response. Unfortunately, the church's response was often agitated rather than strong, reactionary rather than considered.

My aim in this book is to ask, as to each of these seven controversial books, what the big fuss was all about. Who was the author, where did his ideas originate, what did he actually claim, why was the church so upset, and how did it respond? Each chapter begins with a short vignette relating the book's ideas to a concrete event in the world and concludes with some thoughts on the continuing relevance of the book's themes to issues concerning the church today. Although many of the immediate disputes have long since passed—no one is still upset about claims that the earth revolves around the sun—the conflict between each of the seven books and the church continues to cast shadows on beliefs within the church and beliefs about the church within the world.

These seven books will surely not be the last to draw Christian ire. This book argues that since the church has tended to respond poorly to such disfavored literature, then it is incumbent on Christians to learn from their past errors and ponder a more constructive path of engagement with offensive books in the future. As historian George Santayana famously said, those who cannot remember the past are condemned to repeat it.

BOOKS AND IDEAS

This is a book about books, but it is also a book about ideas. Each of the works studied in this volume also stands for some abstract philosophy, most of which can be identified by an "ism." In the pages ahead we will encounter Gnosticism, empiricism, Enlightenment rationalism, evolutionism, communism, psychoanalysis, and postmodernism. The particular books examined will, in almost every case, stand in for a wider set of writings, assertions, practices, and attitudes with which the church has had to contend.

But there is also something distinctive about these books that makes them worth examining in isolation from the wider social currents and ideas they embody. A book has a particular author—a man or woman who is both more specific and more general than any idea. Unlike an abstract principle, an author can be personally demonized and his human frailties exploited as evidence of the book's corruption—because every book is, at some level, autobiographical, a writing that embodies the blood, sweat, and tears of a particular person. Books bring ideas to concrete form and can be thus proven concretely wrong in matters large or trivial. Unlike ideas, books can be banned, burned, or buried. And, as we shall see, sometimes books that were buried make dramatic reappearances to kick-start the controversy anew.

A ROADMAP

Chapter 1 begins in the sands of Egypt, where an extraordinary discovery in 1945 leads to the resurrection of some second-century Gnostic gospels that had been hastily buried after an ecclesiastical ban and hidden for fifteen hundred years. The chapter brings to light a second-century Christian, Valentinus of Alexandria (who nearly became the pope) and his short tract *The Gospel of Truth*, which eventually was condemned as heretical. Since Gnosticism has recently enjoyed resurgence in popular culture, it is well worth understanding what it was all about and why the church found it so alarming.

Chapter 2 shifts from the Middle East to Europe and the story of Galileo Galilei, a seventeenth-century Renaissance man whom the Catholic Church forced to recant the theory that the earth goes around the sun. The chapter examines Galileo's *Dialogue Concerning the Two Chief World Systems*, which provoked the church's ire not only because of its scientific theory but also because of its assault on the authority of the pope over scientific matters and its political threat to the Counter-Reformation. Galileo has become a synecdoche for the church's ignorant suppression of science, a reputation the church has found hard to shake.

Voltaire's *Candide*, studied in chapter 3, is a work of fiction, but its pointed satirical statements about the church were received as anything but idle fancy by eighteenth-century religious authorities. Widely banned as blasphemous and indecent, *Candide* went on to play a major role in the French Revolution and the emerging European tradition of rationalistic religious skepticism that has characterized the continent ever since.

Charles Darwin's extraordinary worldwide tour on *HMS Beagle* and the theory of evolution by natural selection it inspired comprise the subject matter of chapter 4. The church's ferocious assault on Darwinism—which in many ways continues to this day—arguably represents the leading model of how *not* to respond to disfavored books. By insisting that evolution was equivalent to atheism, the church set itself up for the claim—now asserted by leading intellectuals—that scientific proof of evolution is also scientific disproof of God.

Karl Marx's *Communist Manifesto*, examined in chapter 5, laid the foundation for one of the looming totalitarian ideologies of the twentieth century—communism. The American church rallied against Marxism, helping to set up the Cold War morality play between the Christian-capitalist West and the atheist-Communist East. With the demise of the Soviet Union, Marxism seemed to go into remission, but its influence has arguably become deeply embedded in various contemporary ideologies and postmodern identity politics. A fresh examination of Marx's original arguments and their conflicts with Christian belief is as important now as ever.

In conjunction with developing his clinical technique of psychoanalysis, the Austrian psychiatrist Sigmund Freud wrote a number of works that denigrated religion, reducing faith to a psychiatric coping mechanism. Chapter 6 examines his 1927 work *The Future of an Illusion*, in which Freud most comprehensively and forcefully laid out his critique of religious beliefs as illusions buffering man's fear of death. It was easy for Christians to dismiss Freud as a sickened old satyr, particularly because of Freud's shocking interpretations of human sexuality. Yet Freud's longstanding influence on psychology and social science more generally makes it hard to dismiss his work without a considered answer.

In 1988, millions of viewers tuned in for journalist Bill Moyers' PBS interview of Joseph Campbell, whose writings are the subject of chapter 7. In those interviews, Campbell, a leading comparative mythologist, explained the ideas he first articulated in his 1949 book *The Hero with a Thousand Faces*. Campbell purported to show that all world religions were part of a "Monomyth"—a single, universal story of the "hero's journey." The implication, which Campbell was not shy about stating, was that there was nothing distinctive about the Christian story and that it should be taken figuratively rather than literally. Christians have tended to dismiss Campbell as a "new age" kook, but the cultural influence of Campbell's work has been profound. The hundreds of millions of viewers of the *Star Wars* movies have witnessed his handiwork directly, and the idea that Christianity is just another story has become deeply lodged in popular culture.

We conclude in an eighth chapter with some overarching observations on lessons learned from the church's encounter with these seven offending books and with thoughts about more constructive methods of engagement in the future. My goal is not merely to chide the church for a censorial, self-righteous, and ineffective response to books it disfavored. In the coming pages, we shall also encounter examples of positive and successful Christian engagement with worldly scholarship—responses driven by faith, hope, and love rather than fear. It is fear, after all, that drives a dog to bite and fear that drives the censors, book-burners, and name-callers of the world. Christians have nothing to fear from books. The seven books studied here may have rocked the church's walls but could never shake its One Foundation.

CHAPTER 1

Valentinus's *Gospel of Truth*:
Who Doesn't Love a Gnostic
Conspiracy Theory?

"Through the hidden mystery Jesus Christ enlightened
those who were in darkness because of forgetfulness."

Valentinus (or his followers)
The Gospel of Truth (c. AD 140–180)

In December 1945, two brothers from the town of Nag Hammadi in Upper Egypt saddled their camels and went off to dig for fertilizer for their crops.[1] At al-Tarif, a mountain with more than one hundred fifty ancient caves, many previously used as grave sites, the brothers dug into the soft soil. Their tools hit something hard near a large boulder. It was an enormous red earthenware jar, three feet tall.

The superstitious brothers hesitated to open the jar, fearing that a *jinn* or (evil spirit) might dwell inside. But a greedy suspicion that the jar might contain gold eventually outweighed their fear of a *jinn*, and the brothers smashed the jar open. To their disappointment, it contained only books—three ancient leather-bound papyrus books, to be exact. The brothers carried the books home and dumped them near the oven. There, many of the papyri ended up as kindling in the oven as the brothers' mother helped herself to the ready fuel source. And, if Fortune or the Good Lord had not directed things otherwise, the entire set of papyri might have gone up in smoke and the story ended there—as no story at all.

But among the many strange and, to the skeptical mind, random twists of fate that have befallen stigmatized books over the centuries, what happened next ranks as the most fortuitous. Shortly before the brothers set out on that December day, their father had been brutally murdered by one Ahmed Ismail. Now, seeing an opportunity for vengeance, the brothers seized Ismail and "hacked off his limbs . . . ripped out his heart, and devoured it among them, as the ultimate act of blood revenge."[2] This horrifying act of murder and cannibalism has no direct bearing on our story, except that it provided the impetus for the surviving papyri to leave the brothers' home. Fearful that the police investigating the murder would search their home and, in the process, find their scrolls, the brothers entrusted the scrolls to a local Coptic priest. This, in turn, created the opportunity for a local schoolteacher to see the scrolls. The schoolteacher recognized that the scrolls might be valuable and sent them to a friend in Cairo to determine their significance. Eventually, most of the scrolls escaped the black market— how is its own extraordinary story—and made their way to Egyptian Department of Antiquities, which opened them up to the world.

As biblical scholars and historians began to learn of the Nag Hammadi find, they reacted with astonishment. The cache consisted of fifty-two texts written in Coptic and dating to about the third or fourth centuries AD. The Coptic texts were translations of much earlier Greek texts, some of which could not have been much later than the mid-second century AD. Some scholars even believe that some of the original Greek texts were written in the first century, perhaps even before the Gospels of Matthew, Mark, Luke, or John.

But it was the content of the texts, not their mere antiquity, that precipitated so much scholarly excitement. As scholars quickly recognized, the Nag Hammadi texts were a treasure trove of early Christian writings representing an alternative to what eventually became orthodox Christianity. These mostly Gnostic writings apparently presented a long-concealed secret tradition that could rock incumbent Christian doctrines and historical narratives. For instance, when the Dutch historian of religion Gilles Quispel opened one scroll in Cairo, he gasped at the following: "These are the hidden sayings that the living Jesus spoke and Judas Thomas the twin recorded."[4] Secret words of Jesus? Written down by Jesus' twin? Further Nag Hammadi writings called into question other foundational Christian beliefs; for example, by suggesting that Jesus was married to Mary Magdalene and dismissing belief in the virgin birth and bodily resurrection as naive misunderstandings of the shrouded truth.

Not all of the Nag Hammadi texts were previously unknown to Bible scholars. Some had already been discovered, but often in fragmentary form. For example, the "secret words" passage from which Quispel incredulously read came from the *Gospel of Thomas*, fragments of which had been discovered prior to the Nag Hammadi find. But many of the manuscripts were known, if at all, only from dismissive words of early church fathers—(such as Tertullian, Irenaeus, and Hippolytus—)who wrote of heretics and heresies in the church that they were working to suppress. What had previously been seen in only fragmentary form in the mouths of its harshest critics could now been seen fully and directly.

This observation sheds light on the question of why the books had been buried in the ground and hidden to the world for fifteen hundred years. Scholars believe that the scrolls were possibly hidden in the fifth century by a monk from the nearby monastery of St. Pachomius after the church outlawed all gnostic writing and ordered the destruction of all gnostic texts. Perhaps the monk was a gnostic himself, or a sympathizer. Or perhaps he was someone of a scholarly disposition who could not bear to see such a rich collection of ideas lost to history.

Whatever the circumstances of their hiding, one could hardly have scripted a more sensational story for the explosive reintroduction of Gnosticism than that of the rediscovery of the Nag Hammadi scrolls. The rediscovery story performed all of the major themes of orthodox Christianity's confrontation with Gnosticism—secret knowledge, suppression, illumination, bodily resurrection from the earth, and down to the grotesque act of cannibalism eerily reenacting earlier battles over the meaning of the Eucharist. And it set the stage for a renewed contest in scholarly writings and the popular mind over authentic Christian tradition. Does orthodox Christianity represent the "true faith" that won out by God's grace against heretical assault? Or, as Dan Brown would famously claim in his best-selling novel *The Da Vinci Code*, is what we now know as orthodox Christianity merely the winners' version, with another perhaps more authentic strand concealed and suppressed by a multi-millennium ecclesiastical conspiracy?) *whew!*

Among the Nag Hammadi scrolls was a short manuscript called *The Gospel of Truth*. Its author is not identified, but scholars believe it was written either by followers of one Valentinus of Alexandria or by Valentinus himself. As heretical books go, *The Gospel of Truth* doesn't rank with some other Nag Hammadi writings in shocking the sensibilities of modern Christians. There aren't any bombshell revelations about Jesus' twin brother or wife. Modern readers may mostly yawn at the gospel's inscrutable prose. But, among all of the Nag Hammadi writings, the theological and religious vision of the *Gospel of Truth* may have posed the greatest threat to the orthodox tradition: for Valentinus, the man who either wrote or inspired the text, came within a hair's breadth of becoming the bishop of Rome—the pope.[5] Had that occurred, one can only guess at how different the course of church history might have looked.

A HERETIC WHO ALMOST BECAME THE POPE

The great limitation in writing about Valentinus is that we know very little about his personal biography except for what we learn in dismissive comments from people who considered him a dangerous heretic, which is a bit like trying to reconstruct a biography of Washington solely by interviewing King George III. Still, historians have pieced together a plausible profile of the man whose teachings nearly sent the church in a very different direction than the one it ultimately took.[6]

Valentinus was born in Egypt somewhere near the beginning of the second century AD, about a hundred years after the birth of Christ. He received his education at Alexandria, which was then the intellectual capital of the world. Young Valentinus was thoroughly schooled in Greek and Egyptian thought, and he likely had significant exposure to philosophical and religious influences from the East—an important factor in the development of gnostic thought. Alexandria was home to the greatest library the world had ever known and also to a variety of smaller, private libraries that specialized in mystical arts.

Christianity had made its way to Alexandria by time of Valentinus's infancy, but to worldly Alexandrians it must have seemed to be merely a young and disorganized cult. As noted by G. R. S. Mead, an early twentieth-century scholar and prominent member of the Theosophical Society, Valentinus would have experienced Christianity without a canonical New Testament, established catechisms, systematic theologies, or organized hierarchical structures.[7] There would have been a Pauline community imported from Asia Minor, but also a variety of alternative oral traditions and syncretic schools. In this world of primordial Christianity, claims of apostolic authority—that is, a direct connection to Jesus himself—would have been the currency of prestige within the church. Valentinus understood this well, claiming to have been a protégé of one Theodas, an allegedly "apostolic man," of which modern historians know little. It seems likely that, in Alexandria, Valentinus would have encountered the early gnostic teacher Basilides, who claimed to have inherited his teachings from the apostle Matthew and taught for some time in the East among the Persians.

Although we don't know exactly how or why, Valentinus made his way to Rome somewhere around AD 138 and remained there for at least fifteen years, perhaps until around AD 160. According to some historical accounts, he died in Cyprus, driven to insanity and heresy after being shipwrecked. That account is in some tension with other accounts, like that of the church father Tertullian, who claimed that Valentinus was driven to heresy when his own pretensions to becoming Bishop of Rome were thwarted—a subject to which we will return momentarily. Some historians believe that Valentinus eventually made his way back to his roots in Alexandria, ending his life in quiet scholarship.

Little survives of Valentinus's writings, but it appears that he was prolific and exquisitely talented—composing psalms, hymns, and philosophical treatises. Third-century Christian theologian Hippolytus of Rome records a tantalizing fragment from a metrical hymn written by Valentinus that rings of Plato: "I behold all things hanging from air; I perceive all things upheld by spirit; Flesh hanging from soul; Soul standing forth from air; and air hanging from æther."[8] This poetical vignette of a hierarchy of celestial beings with the material world barely hanging on at the lowest rung is characteristic of contemporary gnostic depictions.

At some point during his stay in Rome, Valentinus was apparently in line to become Bishop of Rome, which would have put him at the head of what we now call the Roman Catholic Church. One can easily get the wrong impression when thinking of Valentinus as almost-pope, since the bishops of Rome prior to Emperor Constantine's legalization of Christianity in the Edict of Milan (AD 313) were often obscure characters, who did not yet wield the immense power that came from sitting atop the established church. The second-century church was still decentralized, fragmented, and grasping for its creeds and organizational form. On the other hand, it is precisely that plasticity in the second-century church's character that makes Valentinus's near-miss with the papacy so intriguing. If many of the church's doctrines and beliefs and much of its organizational structure remained up for grabs, a brilliant and forceful leader—which even Valentinus's critics have admitted he was—could have placed a lasting imprint on the church in a way that later popes could not.

To be sure, this is not how all of Valentinus's critics saw it. To the contrary, leading heresiologists (Christian writers responding to heretics) asserted that Valentinus was an orthodox Christian until he lost his bid for the papacy, and that he then turned to heresy in bitterness. Listen, for example, to the church father Tertullian:

> Valentinus had expected to become a bishop, because he was an able man both in genius and eloquence. Being indignant, however, that another obtained the dignity by reason of a claim which confessorship had given him, he broke with the church of the true faith. Just like those (restless) spirits which, when roused by ambition, are usually inflamed with the desire of revenge, he applied himself with all his might to exterminate the truth; and finding the clue of a certain old opinion, he marked out a path for himself with the subtlety of a serpent.[9]

Maybe or maybe not. Charges that a heretic turned from the faith because he couldn't make it in the church were common in orthodox Christian writing.[10]

Although we know about Valentinus only from his critics, we can cross-examine his critics' statements against themselves to see if another story might be right. Among other things, we get differing accounts as to when Valentinus "went heretical," with some authorities insisting that he remained an orthodox Christian for years after he left Rome and others insisting that he became a heretic much earlier.[11] Some scholars conjecture that Valentinus developed his system of thought in Alexandria before coming to Rome and came to the Eternal City for the purpose of disseminating them in the emerging center of Christianity.[12] Certainly, the body of fragmentary writings we have from Valentinus suggest a consistent gnostic orientation throughout his time as a writer. If, in fact, Valentinus was already propagating gnostic ideas during his time in Rome *and* he actually came close to securing the papacy, then the implications for the development of early church doctrine and theology are significant. Some historians argue that the ideas displayed in the *Gospel of Truth* represent a strand of early Christian thought that came close to winning the church.

However close Valentinus came to winning the papacy, there can be little doubt that his influence was significant. He, more than any other person, brought the gnostic challenge to center of Christendom. We know this in part by the extraordinary energy that early Christian writers devoted to refuting his claims. Tertullian informs us that, by the time he took up his quill to rebut Valentinus, four other orthodox paladins had already mounted a charge against the Alexandrian.[13] Church father Irenaeus devoted the entire first book of his five-volume treatise to debunking Valentinianism, demonstrating if not respect at least concern over Valentinus's dramatic influence.

Until 1945, the modern world knew Valentinus's ideas only in fragmentary form or as characterized (or mischaracterized) by his detractors. There were rumors that Valentinus had composed "a gospel," but its text was lost. With the discovery of the Nag Hammadi texts and the *Gospel of Truth*, Valentinus's lost gospel appears to have been rediscovered. Whether Valentinus or one of his followers was the actual author of the precise text of the *Gospel of Truth* is unknown; that the text was heavily based on Valentinus's teaching is certain. Irenaeus informs us that "those who are from Valentinus" boasted to having "more Gospels" than the canonical ones, going to "such a pitch of audacity . . . as to entitle their comparatively recent writing 'the Gospel of Truth,' thought it agrees in nothing with the Gospels of the Apostles, so that they have really no Gospel which is not full of blasphemy."[14] Clearly, Valentinus had struck a nerve.

GNOSIS OR ILLUMINATION

Before examining the text of the *Gospel of Truth*, a few words on the school of thought in which it lies: Gnosticism. Many different sub-schools of Gnosticism have risen (and fallen) over time and place, from several centuries before Christ in India and the East, to the Middle Eastern and Western schools that vied with orthodox Christianity during the Patristic era, to more contemporary influences. The common core of gnostic belief is a dualistic juxtaposition between the material and spiritual worlds. Gnostics reject the human body and physical nature as corruptions or products of evil—the creations of a false god or "Demiurge." The goal of religious teaching is to achieve *gnosis*—or illumination—which allows the believer to escape the material world. This *gnosis* is generally understood to be hidden knowledge, available only to a select few through secret initiation rites.

Gnosticism in the early centuries after Christ often expressed itself in Christian terms with Jesus in the center; although other forms of Jewish Gnosticism also prevailed, such as a Samaritan variety with Simon Magus as the redeemer.[15] The *Gospel of Truth* is one of several "gnostic gospels" found at Nag Hammadi (and elsewhere).[16] Unlike the canonical Gospels, it does not narrate Jesus' life or directly disclose Jesus' teachings. Its structure is more that of a homily or sermon than a history or systematic theology. It is a short book, about fifty-five hundred words, which makes it considerably sparer than Paul's Epistle to the Romans.

The *Gospel of Truth* begins by announcing that "the gospel of truth is joy for people who have received grace from the Father of truth, that they might know him through the power of the Word."[17] In seeming consistency with the opening lines of the Gospel of John, *Truth* asserts that "the Word" is equivalent to "the Savior," but then presents a subtle variation on John's assertion that the Word was present in the beginning and was with God and was God. According to *Truth*, "The Word has come from the fullness in the father's thought and mind" (36), suggesting that Jesus emanated from God as a creative act—an assertion that the Council of Nicaea would emphatically repudiate in AD 325 when it insisted, in response to the Arian controversy, that Jesus was "begotten" but not "created."

Truth turns next to the question of origins. In contrast to the book of Genesis, which has God creating a good world subsequently corrupted by sin, *Truth* has the material world springing from error in the spiritual world. Recognizing the universal desire to know "the

one from whom [you] have come forth," *Truth* delivers the bad news
that we sprang from "ignorance of the Father" that brought about
"terror and fear," which then "grew dense like a fog" until it took the
shape of the material world (36). Humanity thus inhabits a realm
that was initially the product of error and has now given way to ignorance and forgetfulness of the truth.

The modern reader might be curious about what sorts of ethereal beings were supposedly around to cause this error and thus pre-
cipitate the world's creation. Although *Truth* does not flesh out its
assumed cosmology, we know from other writings that Valentinus
and related gnostic writers believed in a complex chain of celestial
beings that overlays the specific Valentinian claims encountered in
Truth. In this chain, each being hangs from the next one up in a long
celestial trapeze. It starts with the Father, God beyond Being, from
whom hangs the Pleroma, the world of living ideas or ideal forms in
Platonic speak. From Pleroma hangs Horos, the Great Boundary or
curtilage of the heavenly sphere. Sophia, or Wisdom, hangs to Horos,
and the Demiurge—the portal to the material world and antagonist
of God beyond Being—clings to her.[18]

Truth's account of material origins sets the stage for the core claim
of Gnosticism—that man's core problem is ignorance of that fact he
lives in a world of illusory materiality and that Jesus came in order
to bring enlightenment and to allow those with this *gnosis* or secret
knowledge to escape the material world: "Through the hidden mystery Jesus Christ enlightened those who were in darkness because of
forgetfulness. He enlightened them and showed the way, and that
way is the truth he taught them" (37). In reaction, Error—now per-
sonified as the enemy—persecuted Jesus and nailed him to a tree in
order to subvert his message of enlightenment. But Jesus' crucifixion
didn't bring the destruction that Error intended. Instead, for those
who partook of the "fruit of this tree," it caused their very lives "to
come into being" (37).

Readers familiar with the Genesis account of humanity's fall
might recognize the inversion of the story of the tree of the knowledge of good and evil. Like that tree, the cross generated a kind of
forbidden fruit, except now those who ate of *this* fruit would find the
very enlightenment forbidden to them in the Genesis account and so

find life rather than death. Subtly, in veiled, flowery language, *Truth* was standing the orthodox worldview on its head.

It followed from this understanding of who Jesus was that the purpose of Jesus' birth, ministry, and death was not, as the orthodox Christian account had it, to offer a substitutionary atonement for sin and thereby achieve reconciliation with God. Rather, Jesus should be understood as a guide and teacher, a wise man always "busy in places of instruction," always refuting the foolish (37). *Truth* does not deal directly with Jesus' resurrection, but it seems by omission to hold the matter irrelevant. In a bastardized paraphrase of Philippians 2, the gospel observes that Jesus "humbled himself even unto death," knowing that "his death would be life for many." And the conclusion: "Oh, what a great teaching!" (38). Jesus' death was a teaching, not atonement. Jesus' ministry and death, not his resurrection, was the whole point of his coming, since it showed the way out of the error and confusion of the material world.

What follows for the gnostic Christian? In opposition to the orthodox Christian account of personal salvation through repentance of sin and belief in Christ, *Truth* teaches that salvation comes through receiving the knowledge of the truth shown by Jesus: "After [Jesus' persecutors] came the little children, who have knowledge of the Father. When they gained strength and learned about the expressions of the Father, they knew, they were known, they were glorified, they gave glory" (37). It was such people who had received enlightenment and escaped error that would find their names written in the book of life. *Truth* portrays this enlightenment version of salvation as that which will ultimately bring the destruction of the material world:

> As one's ignorance about another vanishes when one gains knowledge, and as darkness departs when light comes, so also deficiency disappears in completeness. From then on the world of appearance will no longer be evident, but rather it will disappear in the harmony of unity. (40)

Finally, what were the practical consequences of this teaching for how enlightened ones should lead their lives? *Truth* gestures in the direction of conventional charity: "Steady the feet of those who stumble and extend your hands to the sick. Feed the hungry and give rest to the weary" (43). It also nods in the direction of some degree of evangelization in the sense of teaching others Jesus' secret message, although apparently only those already searching for the truth: "Awaken those who wish to arise and rouse those who sleep, for you embody vigorous understanding" (43). But, mostly, the gospel advocates inward, reflective piety: "Focus your attention upon yourselves. Do not focus your attention upon other things—that is, what you have cast away from yourselves" (43). In the gnostic vision of the *Gospel of Truth*, those escaping from the material world through mystical enlightenment should not get bogged down with the things of the world.

CLASHES WITH ORTHODOXY

Many aspects of the *Gospel of Truth*'s theological challenge to what would become orthodox Christianity are readily apparent on the surface of the text. In contrast to the canonical Gospels' narrative in which Jesus, always existent as the Son of God, was born, died, and rose again to restore humanity's rightful relationship with God in his created world marred by sin, *Truth* imagines the material world as entirely corrupt and illusory and Jesus as a moral teacher who taught and died in order to provide instruction on the method of escape from materiality. Sin, in Valentinus's account, was not the product of Adam's willful disobedience, but rather of ignorance. Salvation came not through repentance but enlightenment.

Some aspects of the *Gospel of Truth*'s challenge to orthodox Christianity are less apparent on the face of the gospel and need to be understood with reference to the fuller body of Valentinian writings, most of which we no longer have. When the early church fathers wrote against Valentinus, they typically wrote against the entire body of teaching, belief, and practice associated with Valentinus and his followers. Often, we can discern shades of these teachings in the *Gospel of Truth*, although it is not always certain whether the secondhand representation of Valentinian thought is fully accurate.

According to Tertullian, for example, Valentinus denied the full manhood of Christ, since that would entail Christ fully entering the illusory realm of materiality. Tertullian charged that, to Valentinus, Christ "was not in the substance of our flesh; but, bringing down from heaven some spiritual body or other, passed through the Virgin Mary as water through a pipe, neither receiving not borrowing aught thence."[19] Tertullian also charged Valentinus with denying the resurrection of the flesh, asserting instead a resurrection of "some sister-flesh." These theological assertions are not directly presented in the *Gospel of Truth*, but they resonate with its text.

Related to these theological challenges was a question of scriptural authority. The New Testament canon remained in flux in the second-century church, with many different texts vying for recognition as authoritative; canonicity remained unresolved until the ecumenical councils of the fourth to eighth centuries. New "gospels" purporting to rest on apostolic authority threatened to destabilize the process of cementing the canon, particularly when those gospels seemed to undermine the historical and theological narratives of the canonical Gospels. Thus Irenaeus complained bitterly that the *Gospel of Truth* contradicted the gospels "handed down to us from the apostles," which "alone are true and reliable and admit neither an increase nor diminution."[20] Similarly, Tertullian complained that Valentinus approved only selectively of "the law and prophets" and had his own gospel, in competition with "these of ours" (meaning the canonical Gospels).[21]

Hippolytus of Rome went even further, accusing Valentinus of condemning "all the prophets and the Law" as "foolish and knowing nothing" and as the "inspiration of the Demiurge, a foolish god."[22] This was a most serious charge, since it suggested that Valentinus was not only making up New Testament books but throwing out the entire Old Testament—an accusation that some modern scholars doubt.[23] It also suggested that Valentinus equated the Old Testament God with the Demiurge, the progenitor of error. To put the point most starkly, orthodox Christians accused Valentinus of calling the God of Abraham, Isaac, and Jacob, Yahweh himself, the source of error and sin—not our savior but the one from whom we needed saving. Such a claim clearly did not sit well with early church fathers, who were in the process of constructing a theology of continuity between the Old and New Testaments.

Modern orthodox Christians view the church's clashes with Gnosticism through the lens of heresy versus the True Faith, with the Truth Faith ultimately winning through God's sovereign grace. Secular scholars, however, often frame these early church theological disputes as being concerned not only with abstract spiritual questions but also with concrete, immediate questions of politics, power, and social organization. The view that Gnosticism and orthodoxy represented two competing and equally "authentic" early Christian traditions concerned as much with earthly matters as with spiritual ones was widely popularized by Princeton professor of religion Elaine Pagels in her 1979 *New York Times* best-seller *The Gnostic Gospels*. Drawing from the Nag Hammadi trove, Pagels argues that gnostic and orthodox Christians clashed along a number of theological dimensions with direct practical implications. Because these claims by Pagels and other scholars have received such wide attention, it is worth examining them in some detail.

For starters, Pagels argues that debates between the gnostics and orthodox over bodily resurrection cannot be understood if examined solely for their "religious content"; the debate must be understood in terms of its "practical effect on the Christian movement."[24] The doctrine of resurrection served "an essential political function" by legitimizing "the authority of certain men who claim to exercise exclusive leadership over the churches as the successors of the Apostle Peter." The gnostics rejected bodily resurrection in favor a spiritual interpretation, which allowed any gnostic "who [saw] the Lord through inner vision" to claim equal authority with the apostles.[25] To put it more generally, according to Pagels, the orthodox argued for bodily resurrection because it allowed them to create a centralized, hierarchical organizational and authoritative structure for the church, and the gnostics argued against bodily resurrection precisely in order to prevent that from happening.

Similarly, Pagels finds political significance in gnostic-orthodox disputes over monotheism. As we have seen, Valentinus could be understood to argue that the Old and New Testament gods were different persons. The orthodox considered such claims blasphemous, Pagels asserts, in large part because they challenged the hierarchical vision of a chain of authority beginning in one God and descending down to all men through a single bishop—the pope. Further, by stressing religion as knowledge rather than practice, "Gnosticism . . . included a religious perspective that implicitly opposed the development of the kind of institution that became the early catholic church."[26]

Gnostic-orthodox disputes over the nature of God also had important social implications for the place of women, Pagels argues.

The Nag Hammadi scrolls contain many passages suggesting an elevated role for women, such as depictions of the Holy Spirit as a mother and the handing down of a secret tradition from Jesus through Mary Magdalene, sometimes identified as Jesus' lover or wife. Valentinus himself identified Sophia or Wisdom as a woman, and her as the creator of the Demiurge, hence literally the Mother of God (or should we say "god"?). The orthodox, by contrast, insisted on continuing the male identity of the Old Testament God, with the effect of subordinating women in the church and the home. Pagels sees these theological disputes over gender as reflecting social contestation in the Greek, Roman, and Jewish worlds over the role of women. Orthodoxy, winning out, confined women to a subordinate role for hundreds or thousands of years to come, writes Pagels.

Finally, Pagels argues that the orthodox belief in Jesus' full humanity and suffering in the flesh contrasted with the gnostic belief in Jesus' essentially spiritual nature and essentially symbolic nature of his passion. This, in turn, had important consequences for how Christians should face persecution. Orthodox Christians welcomed persecution unto death, since it allowed them to follow in the steps of Jesus. The gnostics, by contrast, generally argued that Christians should escape persecution if they could, since it was spiritual insight rather than any act of the illusory flesh that brought salvation. Pagels explains that "Valentinians considered the martyr's 'blood witness' to be second best to the superior, *gnostic* witness to Christ," a view that explains Irenaeus's angry accusation that the gnostics "show contempt" for the martyrs.[27] Pagels thinks that, paradoxically, the orthodox affinity for martyrdom was one of the decisive factors in its eventual triumph over Gnosticism, since it gave the orthodox powerful recruiting propaganda and eventually facilitated their efforts to achieve a bureaucratically organized church.

Whether one finds Pagels' account satisfying depends in large part on one's prior beliefs about Christianity. If one begins with an external view in which Christianity is just another social phenomenon—like the rise of agriculture or democracy—to be studied sociologically, politically, and historically, then her account may be compelling. But if one begins with the premise that the Bible as we have it is the revealed word of God, then the conflict between Valentinus and the orthodox cannot be understood primarily, as Pagels has it, in terms of contending political and social visions. To the orthodox then, as to the orthodox now, the stakes were truth and falsity, not power and social ordering.

THE CHURCH TAKES IT PERSONALLY

We have already seen that, in addition to rebutting his arguments on the merits of his writing, orthodox writers responded to Valentinus's writings by going after the man himself and his followers. Ad hominem attacks leveled against Valentinus included the assertion that he turned to Gnosticism out of pique after being denied the papacy (Tertullian) and that his Gnosticism was the product of insanity following a shipwreck (Epiphanius). Irenaeus, in particular, linked Valentinus's teachings to moral looseness among his followers. The Valentinians, he wrote, were quick to frequent "heathen festival[s] celebrated in honour of the idols," and even "that bloody spectacle hateful both to God and men, in which gladiators either fight with wild beasts, or singly encounter one another."[28] They were also prone to "yield themselves up to the lusts of the flesh with the utmost greediness," seducing married women and pretending "to live in all modesty" with other women as sisters, only to impregnate them. Irenaeus, it seems, was keen on destroying the moral reputation of Valentinians as well as their doctrines.

The contemporary reader may wonder whether these patristic assaults on the moral reputation of the Valentinians were factually justified. The historical record is too scanty to permit firm conclusions, but even if there were some truth to the allegations, it seems unwise to judge gnostic theology based on the behavior of some gnostics. Consider the truthful charges that could have been leveled against the early church: that it was rife with sexual immorality, including incest (1 Cor. 5), prostitution (1 Cor. 6), and adultery and fornication (Rev. 2), idol worship (1 Cor. 10), bitter quarrels and dissension (1 Cor. 1), and forsaking true love for God (Rev. 2). Would we want orthodox Christian theology to be discredited based on moral and spiritual accusations against the early church? If not, then we should be reticent to dismiss gnostic theology based on one-sided reports about the conduct of some Gnostics.

The church's response eventually went well beyond ad hominem attack. After Emperor Constantine's conversation to Christianity and the Edict of Milan recognizing Christianity as an official religion in the fourth century, church authorities turned from the persecuted to the persecutors. By AD 407, Christianity had become the state religion of the Roman Empire and alternative religious beliefs, from pagan to heretical, were violently suppressed.[29] Possession of books denounced as pagan or heretical was made a criminal offense throughout the empire and all copies of such books were ordered burned. For example, in 367 Athanasius, the archbishop of Alexandria, set out an edict compelling the burning of all gnostic books, which may have led to hiding of the Nag Hammadi collection. Until the discovery of the Nag Hammadi texts, most gnostic teaching was known only through isolated fragments of text and the always scathing and sometimes mischaracterizing recitations of heresiologists—which is just what the orthodox wanted.

But, in the longer run, the church's efforts to destroy Valentinus's personal reputation and to bury his writings may have had the counter-effect of creating sympathy for his cause. By vilifying Valentinus and his followers, and then seeking to destroy his written legacy, the church created fodder for modern historians to characterize it as defensive, mean-spirited, and insecure. Typical are the remarks of Bart Ehrman, a leading religious studies scholar, who writes:

> Whatever one might say about this form of Christianity [Valentinism], I don't think we can call it insincere or wanting of feeling. It is warm and intense, full of joy and passion. Its enemies found it heinous, though, and did their utmost both to destroy it and to sully the reputation of the author.[30]

There is an additional sense in which the orthodox church's assault on Valentinus and other gnostics may have backfired. Much of Gnosticism's ostensible appeal comes from its secrecy and exclusivity: its rituals of initiation, its claims of a secret tradition handed down by Jesus to select followers, and its insistence that *gnosis* was only available to a select few. Gnosticism, by its very terms, appeals to the human conceit to be in on the secret. That appeal was bound to be a challenge for the orthodox in any case. But by suppressing Gnosticism and trying to erase its memory, the church arguably compounded the problem. Now, Gnosticism was not only a secret but such an explosive one that it had to be suppressed on pain of death. This created the classic problem of the forbidden fruit, the banned book. Entire book clubs are dedicated to reading banned books, just because they are forbidden. (My fondest desire for *this* book is that someone will try to ban it!) Because of the church's response, Gnosticism became the forbidden secret—and therefore doubly intriguing as the Nag Hammadi texts resurfaced.

Although Gnosticism may have been abhorrent to orthodox Christians, it arguably did them a favor by providing the impetus to sharpen the expression of their theological and organizational ideas. Speaking of Irenaeus's refutation of Valentinus, German scholar Kurt Randolph notes:

> The gnostics have at least this merit, that they prompted [Irenaeus] to this influential presentation of his ideas, in the course of which, evidently without knowing it, many of their considerations proved to be of use to him, and so have remained in the orthodox system.[31]

Theologian and church historian Adolf von Harnack made a similar point about the gnostics more generally, claiming that they were the "first Christian theologians" since they were the first to provide a systematic interpretation of Christian teaching through the lens of Greek philosophy.[32] To respond to these pro-theologians, the church had to muster its own systematic theology—much of which is the theology orthodox Christians still honor today. (Romans 8:28—that God works all things for the good of those who love him and who have been called according to his purpose—comes to mind.)

In summary, the church responded to Valentinus and his progeny through a mix of substantive refutation, ad hominem attack, and outright censorship. In the long run, only the first prong of this attack proved profitable.

FRONTIERS OF GNOSTICISM

Although Valentinus may have lost his bid to become pope, his influence continued to grow after his passing. As Valentinus admirer G. S. R. Mead wrote, "The influence of Valentinus spread far and wide, from Egypt eastwards to Syria, Asia Minor and Mesopotamia, and westwards to Rome, Gaul, and even Spain."[33] Gnosticism seeped throughout the Roman Empire, contending with orthodoxy for hearts and minds. By the fourth century, orthodoxy had largely prevailed in the increasingly institutional and bureaucratic church. Pagels argues that orthodoxy won out not because it was more faithful to the teachings of Christ but because of the concrete organizational advantages implied by orthodox theology. Secular scholars generally view the orthodox denunciation of Gnosticism as a heresy as "winner's history."

After the triumph of orthodoxy, Gnosticism survived in a small number of relatively isolated movements that claimed Valentinus and other gnostic writers as inspiration. From time to time, gnostic influence would show up in the creeds or rituals of some quasi-Christian movement, such as with the Catharism movement in southern Europe in France from the twelfth to fourteenth centuries and a gnostic revival that occurred in late nineteenth-century France. Contemporary examples include: the *Ecclesia Gnostica*, a mostly American liturgical church founded in the twentieth century; and *Ecclesia Gnostica Catholica*, an international fraternal initiatory organization that includes rites administered by both a priest and a priestess.

Gnosticism's most significant recent legacy, however, has not been in organized religious movements but rather in popular culture where, particularly after the Nag Hammadi discovery, we have seen immense popular demand for a Gnosto-revisionist account of the early church. If nothing else, the suppression of Gnosticism by the Constantinian-era church has made for imaginative conspiracy theories. The popular novelist Dan Brown made a meal of it in his bestselling *The Da Vinci Code*, serving up a modern-day thriller based on the premise that the church created the orthodox version of Christianity for political reasons and has been running a dark conspiracy to suppress Gnosticism, the true faith, ever since. In Brown's account, Constantine elevated Jesus to the status of a pagan demi-god in order to unify the Roman Empire, and therefore he had to suppress the true Jesus—including Jesus' marriage to Mary Magdalene and the bloodline or "Holy Grail" the couple left behind.

Never mind that much of Brown's account was grossly ahistorical and created a version of Gnosticism even the gnostics would not have recognized. Brown claimed that the historical facts underlying his novel were "99%" true. A public increasingly skeptical of organized religion and the Catholic Church was willing to eat it up. That the church *had* suppressed most of the gnostic canon through character assassination and outright censorship didn't help in rebutting Brown's conspiracy theory. After all, if there was nothing to hide, then why did the church try to hide it?

In recent years, Gnosticism has shown up, explicitly or implicitly, in many other aspects of popular culture, some sounding in science fiction. For example, in the 1999 movie *The Matrix*, artificial intelligence spawns a world of machines—a matrix—that traps humanity in false consciousness. Liberation can come only through the knowledge that this material world is an illusion. *The Matrix* was the fourth highest grossing film of 1999. Something in the gnostic account of the human condition continues to resonate with the public.

Post-Nag Hammadi discoveries have further fueled the effort to rewrite the Gospel accounts of Jesus' life and ministry and the meaning of his sacrifice. *The Gospel of Judas*, a gnostic text that came to light even more recently than the Nag Hammadi texts, portrays Judas as a sympathetic disciple who was simply doing the will of Jesus. Contemporary writers have taken up this theme, portraying Judas as the only disciple who really "got it" and hence the true tragic hero of the Christian narrative. For example, in his iconoclastic—most Christians would say heretical—novel *The Gospel According to Jesus Christ*, Portuguese Nobel Laureate José Saramago portrays Judas as the only disciple obedient to Jesus' request that his followers help him in being arrested and crucified in order to fulfill God's plan of obtaining adherents outside the Jewish people. That Saramago's lens was satirical rather than historical will not deter many modern readers from rethinking the moral of the Gospels in light of twentieth-century archaeological discoveries.

The church has had its hands full in rebutting the revived popular interest in Gnosticism, but it's possible that Gnosticism has also subtly manifested itself *within the church*, particularly within American evangelicalism. It's not uncommon to hear theologians and Christian reformers assert that evangelicals have veered too far in the direction of emphasizing an individualistic "born again" experience with Jesus and personal interpretation of Scripture as the exclusive meaning of salvation, in derogation of other important aspects of the Christian faith such as sound theology, participation in community, Christian tradition, obedience to appointed authority, and the role of the church. While these tendencies may not partake of gnostic cosmology per se (I have yet to hear a sermon about the Demiurge), many Christians see shades of Gnosticism in evangelicalism's totalizing emphasis on *personal knowledge* of Jesus.

And it's not just concerned Christians who make such claims. The distinguished Yale humanities scholar Harold Bloom found something gnostic in American Christianity's constant drive for personal knowledge and experience:

> Americans always have had a tendency to quest for the unfindable primitive Christian Church. What they actually seek to restore is not the church of the first Christians, but the primal Abyss, named by the ancient Gnostics as both our foremother and forefather.[34]

Whether or not contemporary Christians would agree with Bloom's descriptive claim or find it disturbing, it does not take much imagination to see parallels between *some* of the controversies between Valentinus and the early church fathers and issues that the church continues to discuss today.

Nag Hammadi didn't cause those issues to be raised in the church. They are inherent in the struggle to work out our faith with fear and trembling, just as they were in the second century after Christ. Though Valentinus was not the first or last to raise these issues, he may have given us a useful lens through which to contemplate them. That his particular claims may have been in error does not make them worthless. If nothing else, reading the gnostic gospels today allows modern Christians to understand mistakes the early church narrowly avoided.

Galileo's *Two Chief World Systems*: A Scandal of Religion, Science, and Politics

"I do not feel obliged to believe that the same God who has endowed us with sense, reason, and intellect has intended us to forgo their use and by some other means to give us knowledge which we can attain by them. He would not require us to deny sense and reason in physical matters which are set before our eyes and minds by direct experience or necessary demonstrations."

Galileo Galilei
Open Letter to Grand Duchess Christina (1615)

On June 22, 1633, an elderly, bearded man knelt painfully before seven cardinal inquisitors in Rome, the capital of the Christian world. Holding a candle, he read a statement prepared for him by the Roman Inquisition:

I Galileo Galilei . . . kneeling before you Most Eminent and Most Reverend Cardinals Inquisitors-General against heretical depravity in all of Christendom, having before my eyes and touching my hands the Holy Gospels, swear that I have always believed, and believe now, and with God's help will believe in the future all that the Holy and Apostolic Church holds, preaches, and teaches. . . . [D]esiring to remove from the minds of Your Eminences and every faithful Christian, this vehement suspicion, rightly conceived against me, with a sincere heart and unfeigned faith I abjure, curse, and detest the [Copernican] errors and heresie, and in general each and every other error, heresy, and sect contrary to Holy Church; and I swear that in the future I will never again say or assert, orally or in writing, anything that might cause a similar suspicion about me . . . so help me God and these Holy Gospels.[1]

According to legend, immediately after uttering these tragic words, Galileo muttered under his breath "*eppur si mouve*" ("still it moves"). He probably didn't. By the time of his recantation before the Inquisition, Galileo was a broken man, repeatedly interrogated and threatened with physical torture. Pope Urban made it known that Galileo's punishment would be "mild" only because of his age and ill health: house arrest for the remainder of his life, censure and prohibition of his famous book, and an obligation to recite the seven penitential psalms weekly for the next three years. Galileo surely still believed that the earth revolves around the sun, but he was in no condition to utter it on that dreadful day.

What had the most distinguished scientist of his day done to merit this treatment? Twenty-three years previously, Galileo had published a tract called *The Starry Messenger* that presented evidence for the Copernican theory of heliocentricism: the earth orbits the sun rather than the other way around, as was generally believed at the time and enshrined in Catholic dogma. The Catholic Church had reacted sternly, prohibiting the teaching of anything other than the Ptolemaic theory that earth is the center of the universe and that all other heavenly bodies orbit the earth. Undaunted, in 1622 Galileo published his *Dialogue Concerning the Two Chief World Systems*, under a printing license from the Inquisition that turned out to be insufficient to spare Galileo from prosecution. *Dialogue* compared the evidence for the Copernican and Ptolemaic systems and left no doubt of the author's belief that the Copernican system had the better side of the argument. Galileo miscalculated politically in publishing the *Dialogue* and soon faced a trial for his life before the Inquisition.

The "Galileo Affair," as it became known, would live on long after the Catholic Church accepted geocentricism and even centuries later after Pope John Paul II seemingly apologized for the church's treatment of Galileo. Over time, it became the incarnate symbol of the view that Christianity and science are incompatible, that scriptural literalism stands in the way of scientific progress, and that the church is run by dangerous and illiberal dogmatists. It became, in short, the one-size-fits-all reference for anyone wanting to tar the church with malicious Luddite-ism.

The question that survives the Galileo Affair—the question that rears its ugly head whenever Christianity seems to run into science—is what it all means. What is the lesson and legacy of the church's quixotic battle against heliocentricism? (Is "the church" writ large to blame, or only certain reactionary elements in the Inquisition? Does the Galileo Affair demonstrate that the Christian faith and scientific discovery are inherently at loggerheads? And, looking forward, how can the church stay true to Scripture and the faith in a world of challenging scientific discovery that sometimes seems to rock the foundations of Christian belief?)

THE TERRESTRIAL LIFE OF A STARRY MESSENGER

Although the name of Galileo Galilei is strongly associated with heliocentricism, he was not the first person to discover that the earth revolves around the sun. That theory was proposed at least as early as Aristarchus of Samos (in the third century BC.) But Aristarchus received relatively little attention in the medieval world, where the prevailing view centered on the geocentric or earth-centered model proposed in the second century AD by Ptolemy of Alexandria, a countryman and contemporary of Valentinus, whom we studied in chapter 1, and on Aristotle's earlier arguments for the perfect and unchanging nature of the heavenly spheres.

In 1543, an obscure Polish mathematician named Nicolaus Copernicus shattered the cosmos with the publication of *De revolutionibus orbium coelestium* (*On the Revolutions of the Celestial Spheres*), a largely mathematical rather than observational proof that the earth revolves around the sun. In the years that followed, astronomers and physicists published new theories of the cosmos that, while inaccurate in large part from the perspective of modern science, laid down further challenges to the prevailing Ptolemaic and Aristotelian views. Around the time of Galileo's birth, Danish nobleman and astronomer Tycho Brahe proposed a blending of the Copernican and Ptolemaic systems with the moon orbiting the earth, the planets orbiting the sun, but the sun orbiting the earth. His junior collaborator, Johannes Kepler, extended Brahe's work, by showing that the supernova of

1604 implied the mutability of the heavenly spheres, thus demolishing Aristotle's theory of a perfect and unchanging heaven.

Europe was thus in the midst of tremendous scientific upheaval—not to mention the continuing religious, political, economic, and military fallout from the Protestant Reformation—when Galileo was born in Pisa in 1564. His father, a musician, stressed the need to test the factual accuracy of harmonic rules, an empiricist bent that exerted a strong influence on Galileo's future career as a scientist. Galileo studied medicine and mathematics in Pisa, eventually securing appointments as a professor of mathematics in Pisa and Padua. Initially, Galileo's research focused primarily on the theory of motion and of falling bodies in particular. The story that he dropped objects from the Leaning Tower of Pisa to test the laws of gravity may well be apocryphal, but Galileo did make important contributions to mathematical understanding, including a close approximation of the law of inertia and the parabolic path of projectiles.

Around 1609, Galileo took up a new professional interest in astronomy. As a mathematician, he was attracted to Copernicus's mathematical demonstration that a moving earth made more sense than a fixed earth. But, as Copernicus's critics frequently pointed out, a moving earth contradicted sensory observation. For example, if the earth were in motion, why wouldn't bodies on its surface be thrown off by centrifugal force? And why wouldn't bodies in free fall follow a slanted rather than vertical path?

So Galileo initially taught Ptolemy in his courses and rebuffed Kepler's efforts to interest him in alternative theories. Then, in 1609, rumors circulated in Italy that Dutch spectacle makers had contrived a gadget that made distant object appear near. The possibility of a telescope had been known for some time, but here, as with the question of heliocentricism, scriptural interpretation may have gotten in the way of scientific progress. Some Catholic leaders believed that seeing things at a distance belonged to the devil's arts, on account of Satan having shown Jesus the distant kingdoms of the world as recorded in Luke 4:5.[2] Galileo himself was initially skeptical that the Dutch gadget would be of much scientific value; but when he finally acquired a specimen and began improving it, the universe changed. Indeed, it exploded.

The best way to follow what occurred next is to hear it in Galileo's own telling. In 1610, Galileo published *Sidereus Nuncius*—usually translated the "Starry" or "Sidereal" Messenger—documenting his recent discoveries with the telescope or "spyglass."[3] Galileo eagerly recounted his construction of a succession of telescopes by fitting off-set concave and convex lenses into a tube and progressively increasing its magnification, eventually allowing the viewer to see objects as though thirty times nearer than by the naked eye. To assist his narrative, Galileo provided a schematic of his telescope, a pattern he continued throughout his book. *Sidereus Nuncius* contains over seventy drawings and diagrams of the moon and constellations such as Orion, Pleiades, and Taurus, and the moons of Jupiter.

Having focused his telescope on the moon, Galileo discovered that it was not a perfectly spherical orb as held by many philosophers, but rather was "full of inequalities, uneven, full of hollows and pro-tuberances, just like the surface of the earth itself" (*SM* 52). Galileo calculated the height of some of the mountains as over four miles—a reasonably accurate calculation. He also observed that the moon receives its light from the sun and that its position relative to the earth and sun determines the moon's phases.

Galileo next recounted what occurred when he turned his telescope to the stars. The heavens came alive, and he was able to discern ten times more stars than with naked-eye observation. Familiar constellations abounded with new stars under the eye of Galileo's invention. For example, Galileo could now make out eighty stars in the constellation Orion, almost nine times the nine stars ordinarily associated with the Hunter. Naked-eye observers could typically see six or seven stars in the Pleiades, but the telescope revealed more than forty additional stars in the constellation. Anyone observing the Milky Way Galaxy through the telescope, he wrote, would instantly see that "all the disputes which have tormented philosophers through so many ages are exploded at once by the indubitable evidence of our eyes, and we are freed from the worldly disputes upon this subject"; the galaxy is "nothing but a mass of innumerable stars planted together in clusters" (*SM* 66). Nebulae, previously believed to be clouds, were simply thick clusters of stars. Galileo provided an illustration of the Nebula of Praesepe—the beehive—to show that it was not a single mass but, in his view, a cluster of forty stars.

By affirming that "evidence of our eyes" trumps philosophical speculation, Galileo had already thrown down the gauntlet to the

Catholic establishment, but he now proceeded to what he "considered the most important [observation] in this work" (*SM* 67). For over two months, Galileo had observed the positions and movements of four new planets—(what we now know to be moons of Jupiter.) What appears for the next fifteen or so pages of *Starry Messenger* is essentially Galileo's observational diary of the four "planets" from January 7 to March 2, 1610. Based on his daily observations (excepting cloudy days, which Galileo dutifully chronicled as unobservable), the moons changed their positions relative to Jupiter from night to night, and yet they always appeared in the same straight line near the planet. Galileo concluded that the moons were orbiting Jupiter. From this, he concluded that his research had uncovered:

> A notable and splendid argument to remove the scruple of those
> who can tolerate the revolution of the planets around the sun in the
> Copernican system, but are so disturbed by the motion of one moon
> around the earth (while both accomplish an orbit of one year's length
> around the sun) that they think this constitution of the universe must
> be rejected as impossible. (*SM* 84)

He didn't claim that the existence of Jupiter's moons proved that the Copernican system was correct (that the earth orbited the sun). He simply asserted that the fact of four moons orbiting Jupiter while Jupiter and its moons orbited the sun showed that a system in which heavenly bodies orbited bodies other than the earth wasn't impossible.

Galileo followed up on *Starry Messenger* with work on the behavior of solid bodies in water and on sunspots, which led him into heated disputation with Aristotelian philosophers. The work on sunspots was particularly significant to Galileo's later work countering the Ptolemaic theory of the earth and sun. Contrary to Aristotelian philosophers who argued that sunspots were little planets, thus preserving the sun's perfection and immutability, Galileo argued that sunspots occurred on the surface of the sun, and that their appearance and disappearance demonstrated that the sun rotated on its axis like the earth. That the sun rotated like the earth and was subject to changeable imperfections presented a serious challenge to the prevailing Aristotelian and Ptolemaic models.

As word of Galileo's Copernican beliefs spread, conservative elements in the Catholic Church began to accuse Galileo of heresy.

Ahead, we shall examine in greater detail the basis for the church's objection to Copernicanism, but the core of the accusation centered on a single passage from the Bible, Joshua 10:12–13, where God stopped the sun to give Joshua time to win a battle over the Amorites. Read literally, this passage suggested that the sun ordinarily moved about the earth, not the earth around the sun.

Acutely aware of the theological obstacles facing his scientific discoveries, Galileo wrote a series of private letters in late 1613 that ended up in wide circulation. Galileo remained a good Catholic throughout his life (if we can put aside his fathering of three illegitimate children) and wanted to vindicate his science in Christian terms. In his letters, Galileo argued the Bible was authoritative on faith and morals but was not a science manual, and that physical observation of the world had to trump interpretation of ambiguous biblical passages when it came to scientific matters. The fires were now burning in Rome and a committee of the Inquisition was formed to study the heliocentricism issue. In December 1615, Galileo traveled to Rome to defend his Copernican views. He achieved only limited success insofar as the Inquisition rebuffed efforts to brand Copernicanism a heresy—which would have been a very serious finding. But Galileo lost more than he gained. In a private audience, Cardinal Robert Bellarmine forbade Galileo to defend the truth of the earth's motion. With little choice, Galileo agreed to comply. Further, the Congregation of the Index published a decree stating that claims that the earth moved were false, and they placed *De revolutionibus* and other Copernican works on the dreaded *Index Librorum Prohibitorum*—the church's list of prohibited books (the Index remained in place until 1966).

At this point, Galileo might have left well enough alone and retreated back to other scientific topics; but the appearance of three comets in 1618 drew him into academic disputation with the Jesuits on such questions as whether the comets traversed the earth's atmosphere (as Aristotle and now the Jesuits claimed) or rather the heavens (which Galileo claimed and which would tend to undermine the heaven/earth dichotomy). Galileo's view flirted dangerously with an endorsement of Copernicanism, but he was emboldened by the election of Cardinal Maffeo Barberini, a friend and admirer of his, as Pope Urban VIII in the summer of 1623. Galileo published another tract, *The Assayer*, defending his view on the comets in the fall of 1623 and dedicated the book to the new pope.

The change in Vatican leadership and Galileo's impunity in publishing *The Assayer* led him to believe that the political climate had turned favorable for further work on a Copernican agenda. By 1632, Galileo, now working in Florence, sought the Inquisition's permission for the publication of a work synthesizing the arguments in favor of geokinesis and showing their superiority over geostatic theories. As we shall see momentarily, Galileo believed that his new work, *Dialogue*, did not violate the injunction against publishing pro-Copernican work, since the book was ostensibly structured as a dialogue between Copernican views on the one hand and Ptolemaic and Aristotelian views on the other. Galileo sought and received a license to print the book in Florence from the chief censor in Rome, a Dominican named Niccolò Riccardi, who actually coauthored the book's introduction with Galileo.

Alas for Galileo in his lifetime and alas for the church's reputation in subsequent centuries, for conservative elements in Rome reacted with fury to the publication of his *Dialogue*. Although the book purported neutrally to showcase dialogue between heliocentricism and geocentricism, anyone could see that Galileo had stacked the decks in favor of heliocentricism. Soon, he faced charges that his book violated both the Index's prohibition on advocating Copernican theories and a personal injunction issued against discussing the earth's motion issued to Galileo in 1616.

Summoned to trial in Rome, Galileo learned that he could not count on his erstwhile friend Pope Urban to bail him out. Being convicted of deliberate insubordination to the church and actual heresy—and condemned to gruesome death—was a real possibility. After a succession of coercive interviews where physical torture was held out as an incentive to cooperate, Galileo finally succeeded in cutting a plea bargain. He would reread *Dialogue* and admit seeing, to his surprise, that he had given the impression that he favored the Copernican view while unconsciously overcompensating the weaker argument—Copernicanism. The Inquisition ultimately found him guilty on a charge of "vehement suspicion of heresy"—not as damning as actual heresy but still a grave finding. And this landed Galileo where we first encountered him, on his knees in Rome, making his humiliating, insincere adjuration.

After five months, Galileo's initial sentence of imprisonment at the hands of the Inquisition was commuted to house arrest at his villa near Florence, where he lived another decade until his death in 1642. One salutary side effect of the otherwise tragic Galileo affair was that the old man went back to work on the subject of his youthful expertise—the physics of motion—leading to the publication of Galileo's most important contribution to physics, *Two New Sciences*, in 1638. Still, he was never again allowed the freedom to travel or to discuss his views on cosmology openly, and he remained subject to the Inquisition's oversight and control until his death.

A RATHER ONE-SIDED "DIALOGUE"

What was so scandalous about Galileo's *Dialogue*? Its introduction, coauthored with Riccardi, begins with a clever, if not cheeky, tip of the hat to the anti-Copernican Decree of the Index of 1616. That decree, asserts Galileo, was "a salutary edict . . . to prevent the dangerous scandals of the present age."[4] Unfortunately, however, there were those outside of Italy who "rashly asserted that the decree was the offspring of an extremely ill-informed passion and not of judicious examination," and that "consultants who are totally ignorant of astronomical observations" had "cut the wings of speculative intellects by means of an immediate prohibition" (*D* 190). Not so, protested Galileo. To the contrary, the Catholic establishment had carefully listened to Galileo's arguments on behalf of Copernicanism before issuing the edict. The *Dialogue* was written to set the record straight—to "show to foreign nations that we in Italy, and especially Rome, know as much about this subject as transalpine diligence can have ever imagined" (*D* 190). In other words, Galileo purported to prove that the Roman censors were not ignorant bumpkins after all, which he would accomplish, paradoxically, by showing the many strong arguments for the Copernican system that the censors had heard and rejected. From a safe vantage point several centuries removed from the Inquisition, Galileo's machinations appear positively comical.

The *Dialogue* is structured as a conversation over four days between two philosophers and a layman, which Galileo explained would permit exploration of a range of topics beyond the purely mathematical.

Salviati, named for Galileo's friend Filippo Salviati, advances the Copernican position. Simplicio argues for the traditional Ptolemaic and Aristotelian principles. Galileo purported to name him after Simplicius of Cilicia, a sixth-century commentator on Aristotle, but he clearly meant mischief. Simplicio is modeled on two contemporary conservative philosophers who opposed Galileo, and Simplicio resonates with *semplice* or "simpleminded." The third participant in the *Dialogue*, Sagredo, is an everyman who starts out neutral but shifts in Salviati's favor as the conversation unfolds, leaving no doubt as to how other laymen should score the debate.

On the first day, the conversants debate the authority of Aristotle, who had argued for the completeness and perfection of the world based on its three dimensions. Much of the argument is scientific in nature, with Salviati questioning the idea of a perfected and immutable universe in light of recent observations of phenomena such as sunspots, lunar mountains, and the appearance of new stars—matters Galileo had covered in *The Assayer*. Simplicio weakly asserts theories that had been created to account for these phenomena, some of which had already been discarded by their creators. The decks were quite clearly being stacked in favor of Salviati.

The second day of the *Dialogue* takes an epistemological turn: Should we believe that Aristotle was right just on the authority of him being Aristotle or because the things he argued were persuasive? Salviati demands:

> Do you have any doubt that if Aristotle were to see the new discoveries in the heavens, he would change his mind, revise his books, accept the more sensible doctrines, and cast away from himself those who are so weak minded as to be very cowardly induced to want to uphold every one of his sayings? (*D* 198)

Arguments from authority cannot stand up to arguments from empirical observations made with our own eyes:

> So, Simplicio, come freely with reasons and demonstrations (yours or Aristotle's) and not with textual passages or mere authorities because our discussions are about the sensible world and not about a world on paper. (*D* 201)

The argument then transitions into scientific theory, with Salviati answering three objections to a moving earth: (1) that the earth would leave behind a falling body, causing the body to land to the west of the point from which it was dropped; (2) that a cannonball fired to the west would fly further than one fired to the east; and (3) and that a cannonball fired vertically would land to the west. Today, we would answer by pointing out that the earth's atmosphere travels with the earth, but Galileo—or rather Salviati—had to answer these objections based on the knowledge of the day, and thus he resorted to Aristotle's theory of impetus, or the force of a moving body.

On the third day, Salviati goes on the attack, presenting evidence from the movement of Mars, Jupiter, and Saturn in relation to the earth that the other planets revolve around the sun. Sagredo, still struggling to decide who's right, brings up other objections from a terrestrial perspective. If the earth rotated, then wouldn't the mountains soon become inverted so that one would have to descend rather than ascend them? But even Simplicio can see that this is no different than circumnavigating the globe, which the Portuguese sailor Fernão de Magalhães and his crew accomplished in 1522. Sagredo also offered the following thought experiment: Suppose you were looking up from the bottom of a well at the night sky. If the earth were moving, wouldn't stars quickly appear and disappear? Galileo challenges Sagredo to ask himself what fraction of the sky could be seen from the well's bottom, suggesting that the answer to Sagredo's puzzle lies in understanding our limited perspective on the heavens.

On the fourth and final day of the *Dialogue*, Salviati presses his obvious advantage based on the movement of the tides in conjunction with lunar phases. Simplicio fumbles for counter-explanations, but eventually he has to fall back on the possibility that aspects of tidal movement are miraculous, hidden by God, and unavailable for discovery by human inquiry. This "God of the gaps" whimper sets up Salviati for a triumphant closing statement. Simplicio's allusion to miracles is "an admirable and truly angelic doctrine, to which there corresponds very harmoniously another one that is divine. That is the doctrine which, while it allows us to argue about the constitution of the world, tells us that we are not about to discover how His hands built it" (*D* 270). This clever allusion to Ecclesiastes 3:10–11, which states that no man can discover the work that God has made from beginning to end, carves neatly the respective theories of science and theology: questions of how God created the world belong to theology; questions of how the world works, to science.

There can be no question as to whether Copernicus or Ptolemy and Aristotle win the debate. Although Salviati purports not to have decided whether the Copernican system is correct, his thorough trouncing of the straw-man Simplicio leaves no doubt as to whom Galileo considers right. At one point, Sagredo puts into context Galileo's daring iconoclasm:

> I begin to believe that when someone abandons an opinion imbibed with mother's milk and accepted by infinitely many persons, and he does this in order to switch to another one accepted by very few and denied by all the schools . . . he must necessarily be moved (not forced) by stronger reasons. (*D* 218)

Let tradition and consensus be forgotten, Galileo says; the evidence against them is overwhelmingly more compelling.

HELIOCENTRICISM (QUITE LITERALLY) ROCKS THE WORLD

Unlike the debate over Darwinism, which still rages on as we shall see in chapter 4, it's difficult for contemporary Christians to understand what could possibly have been so offensive about Galileo's assertion of heliocentricism. One answer is that the Galileo Affair may have had more to do with the politics of Urban's papal court (for example, power struggles between Jesuits and Dominicans) and the perception that Galileo was insubordinate in publishing after being ordered not to do so, than it had with the scientific and theological merits of the debate. Historians continue to debate exactly how to understand the Galileo Affair in terms of the individual personalities, relationships, and institutions of Catholicism that created its historical context.

But the political intrigue surrounding the seventeenth-century Vatican and Galileo's personal conduct do not fully explain the Galileo Affair. There was something problematic about the theory, not just the man. The church's concern with heliocentricism did not originate with Galileo, and the Inquisition considered the matter a serious question of theology. To see why, we need to consider three different dimensions—interpretation, authority, and social meaning—in which the *Dialogue* rocked the church. Each of these dimensions reflected significant fault lines in Christian theology, which were laid bare when Martin Luther allegedly nailed his Ninety-Five Theses to the Wittenberg church door in 1517. Although Copernicus was a devout Catholic and dedicated his *De revolutionibus* to Pope Paul III, Copernicanism emanated from Protestant territory, which to Rome implied Protestant values. The year of Galileo's trial in Rome (1633) fell in the dead center of the Thirty Years' War, in which Protestants and Catholics were killing each other across Europe. Galileo's *Dialogue* struck deep religious-ideological nerves.

First, heliocentricism created a serious question of scriptural hermeneutics, or methods of interpretation. In addition to the Joshua account of God causing the sun to stand still, Catholic authorities marshaled other passages—such as Psalm 19, Psalm 93, and Ecclesiastes 1—in favor of the assertion that the Scriptures taught that the sun moved and the earth stood still. Although contemporary critics often mistakenly attribute the church's prohibition of heliocentricism to biblical literalism, that is an anachronistic view of the problem. Interpretative literalism appeared in later branches of Protestant fundamentalism, not in seventeenth-century Catholicism. The problem was less literal interpretation of the Bible than that the church had built an entire cosmological theology based on its historical interpretation of various scriptural passages suggesting a static earth and mobile sun. Heliocentrism challenged the church's longstanding interpretations of Scripture, at a time when Catholic theology lodged ever greater authority on the interpretative traditions of the church. Cardinal Bellarmine admonished Galileo against advancing scriptural arguments in favor of heliocentricism, since that would "suggest an interpretation of Scripture which is contrary to all the Holy Fathers and to all the Greek and Latin commentators."[5] The heliocentric interpretation of Scripture was new at a time when interpretative novelty was highly disfavored due to clashes with destabilizing Protestant interpretations of Scripture.

Second, perhaps more importantly than the question of *how* the Scriptures should be interpreted was the question of *who* was entitled to interpret them. In its judgment against Galileo, the Inquisition found him guilty of "interpreting Holy Scripture according to [his] own meaning."[6] In Galileo's revolt against the church's conventional interpretation of Scripture as to the order of the cosmos, the Inquisition sniffed a dangerously Protestant odor. Heliocentricists were daring to interpret the Scriptures for themselves in ways contrary to the teachings of church authorities. Wasn't this the very heart of the Reformation problem—the assertion of the priesthood of all believers and the right of lay individuals to draw their own interpretation of Scripture? The Counter-Reformation Council of Trent had sought to stamp out such dangerous individualism, decreeing in the mid-sixteenth century:

> No one relying on his own judgment shall, in matters of faith and morals pertaining to the edification of Christian doctrine, distorting the Scriptures in accordance with his own conceptions, presume to interpret them contrary to that sense which the holy mother Church . . . has held or holds.

If a heliocentric view ever were to be accepted as compatible with Scripture, then such a reform would have to come through proper channels of the church hierarchy. To allow individual Christians to make such judgments smacked of anarchic Protestantism. And yet here was Galileo, a layman, purporting to interpret Scripture his own way to create a license for his scientific theories.

A related point concerns the scope of the church's preemptive jurisdiction over scriptural interpretation. Galileo argued that the church's interpretation on Scripture should be considered authoritative on questions of faith and morals, but not on questions of science. The church demurred. Every interpretation of Scripture by the church was sacrosanct, and every challenge to it heretical. Again, Cardinal Bellarmine: "Thus anyone who would say that Abraham did not have two sons and Jacob twelve would be just as much a heretic as someone who would say that Christ was not born of a virgin."[7] The Galileo Affair thus raised an important question about the breadth of the church's monopoly over scriptural interpretation.

Finally, heliocentricism rocked the church ideologically and politically at a time when it was already feeling tremendous internal and external pressures. The social and political order of the seventeenth century remained heavily hierarchical, and its hierarchy cribbed heavily from the contemporary understanding of the physical universe. God and heaven existed in perfection outside the celestial sphere, and the angels controlled the unchanging and geometrically unblemished celestial sphere. Descending to earth, one continued the slide down the hierarchy into the zone of imperfection where everything and everyone had its place, from the church at the top, to political rulers, to ordinary people, and finally down to the plants and animals. Heliocentrism jeopardized the cosmological hierarchy, with untold implications below on the earth. Even Galileo recognized, in the voice of Simplicio, that "this way of philosophizing tends to subvert all natural philosophy, and to disorder and set in confusion heaven and earth and the whole universe." The stakes for the church were high. Upset the hierarchy of the heavens, and you upset the hierarchy of the earth.

These theological, social, and political friction points remain highly contested four hundred years after Galileo—although not of course in the particular case of heliocentricism. How should the Scriptures be interpreted when they seem to conflict with scientific discoveries? Was Galileo right in arguing that scriptural interpretation should be more flexible and adaptive when it comes to questions of science than on questions of faith and morals, or does such a principle create a species of interpretative relativism that will soon undermine the authority of Scripture altogether? And who is qualified to interpret Scripture on scientific matters? Should pastors and theologians defer to scientists when it comes to understanding Scripture in light of evolving scientific knowledge, or should the meaning of Scripture be determined independently of scientific learning? Such questions continue to simmer today, be it with respect to evolution, genetics, bioethics, or cosmology.

The questions of the social and moral meaning of scientific discovery in relation to Scripture are also as relevant today as they were in seventeenth-century Italy. Ahead, we shall see that anti-Darwinists were as much (or even more) concerned about the social and philosophical implications of Darwinism as with its direct implications for scriptural interpretation. Albert Einstein's relativity theory had a profound effect on philosophical and moral reasoning, arguably fueling postmodernism and moral relativism.

Or, perhaps we should say that new scientific theories have important moral implications if we let them. The linkage isn't inevitable; one could insist, with Galileo, that the domains of science and faith are sealed off from each other. Galileo denied that his cosmology had any implication for faith or morals, and he insisted that scientific inquiry could proceed on a completely separate track from theology. This is one strategy for insulating the heart of the Christian message and practice from the vicissitudes of potentially disturbing scientific theories.

But it is far from clear that such a sharp cleavage is either possible or desirable. The Catholic Church may have been grievously wrong in its treatment of Galileo and heliocentricism, and yet correct in insisting that scientific theories contrary to prevailing interpretations of Scripture can't simply be dismissed as irrelevant to faith and morals. After all, Christians are quick to embrace scientific discoveries that seem to support biblical accounts, be it geologic evidence corroborating Noah's flood or a Big Bang evidencing *ex nihilo* creation. A selective approach of embracing favorable science and dismissing unfavorable science as irrelevant won't sway many wavering souls, nor honestly will it fulfill the admonition to love God with all our minds. Either Scripture and science must let each other alone or they must engage each other for better or for worse.

Galileo's *Dialogue* rocked heaven and earth. Before too long, his scientific claims were no longer controversial and the earth stopped shaking. But the deeper questions he raised of interpretation, authority, and social meaning may be with us always.

THE CHURCH APOLOGIZES

It took some time for the Catholic Church to dig itself out of the Galileo Affair. Books advocating heliocentricism remained on the Index, which meant they were banned for Catholics, until 1758. Even when the church lifted the general heliocentricism injunction, Galileo's *Dialogue* remained prohibited, underlying again the fact that the problems with Galileo's work transcended the particulars of his empirical claims about the earth's movement. It wasn't until 1835, two hundred years after the Galileo Affair, that the church quietly removed all Copernican books from the Index, explaining that the prior finding that Copernicus was "contrary to Scripture" had meant only the traditional understanding of Scripture. Galileo was finally unshackled to speak in the Catholic world.

Throughout the course of the twentieth century, popes and other prominent Catholics have occasionally made positive references to Galileo, suggesting that Galileo had been unfairly tarnished. But it was not until 1979 that Pope John Paul II—like Copernicus, a Pole—raised the question directly of whether the church owed Galileo an apology. John Paul acknowledged that Galileo "had to suffer a great deal at the hands of men and organisms of the church," and he expressed the hope that "theologians, scholars and historians, animated by a spirit of sincere collaboration, will study the Galileo case more deeply and, in loyal recognition of wrongs from whatever side they come." Following up on the pope's admonition, in 1981 a Pontifical Interdisciplinary Study Commission launched an inquiry into the Galileo Affair. The commission's work culminated in a speech by the pontiff in 1992, which recognized again that Galileo had been wronged. Critics have protested that the pope's speech was too equivocal, branding as a "myth" the popular perception that the Galileo Affair showed the church rejecting scientific progress and blaming Galileo for too stoutly defending heliocentricism when it was still an unproven theory.

Despite the pope's acquittal of Galileo, other prominent Catholics have continued to wonder whether the fault was more Galileo's than the church's. In a 1990 speech, Cardinal Joseph Ratzinger, who was then the Prefect of the Sacred Congregation of the Doctrine of the Faith (formerly known as the Inquisition) and the future Pope Benedict XVI, quoted philosopher of science Paul Feyerabend as follows:

> The Church at the time of Galileo kept much more closely to reason than did Galileo himself, and she took into consideration the ethical and social consequences of Galileo's teaching too. Her verdict against Galileo was rational and just, and the revision of this verdict can be justified only on the grounds of what is politically opportune.[8]

Note the emphasis on the "ethical and social consequences" of scientific theories. In this view, scientists have an obligation not just to search for the truth but also to present (or not present) their discoveries with an eye to the collateral of moral consequences. Galileo may have been right in his science but wrong in his morals. Four hundred years after the Galileo Affair, this view remains alive.

SPINNING THE "GALILEO AFFAIR"

As a scientific matter, Galileo's findings were not the last word of course. From a big-picture perspective, heliocentricism—the assertion that the sun was the center of the universe—was only a slight improvement on the claim that everything revolved around the earth. Further observations by William Herschel, Friedrich Bessel, and other astronomers in the nineteenth century showed that the sun was near the center of the solar system but not the universe. And then radical advances in astronomical observation technology and astrophysics began to show that the universe was immensely large, in constant motion, and expanding.

But Galileo's contributions remain immensely important to the process of scientific discovery. Along with his contemporary Sir Francis Bacon, Galileo's name stands in for the proposition that empirical measurement trumps philosophical speculation. What Galileo saw with his own eyes through his telescope could in one sweep displace two thousand years of Aristotelian metaphysics. Measurement, observation, and recordation would become the hallmarks of the Age of Discovery that swept entirely new continents, peoples, animal species, diseases, technologies, and social arrangements into the European eyepiece.

More generally, the Catholic Inquisition's suppression of Galileo has become a charged reference point in ongoing debates over the relationship between Christianity and science. The debates center on whether the Galileo Affair was an unfortunate one-off, understandable for its times and soon remedied, or whether it instead encapsulates a fundamental and perhaps insoluble tension between the church and science. Many atheists and skeptics have taken the view that the Galileo Affair is simply the best-known episode in a continuing clash between Christianity and science that will continue until science finally displaces religious superstition.

An anecdote from a famous contemporary scientist illustrates this point of view. In his best-selling *A Brief History of Time*, physicist Stephen Hawking recounts attending a 1981 Vatican conference in which the pope "told us that it was all right to study the evolution of the universe after the big bang, but we should not inquire into the big bang itself because that was the moment of Creation and therefore the work of God."[9] Hawking rebuffed the pope's admonition because he "didn't want to share the fate of Galileo." Hawking might as well have said, in the immortal words of Ronald Reagan, "There you go again." For many religious skeptics, the specter of Galileo appears every time the church and science have a run-in.

Catholic Christians, in particular, dispute such characterizations. To them, the Galileo Affair was an unfortunate but short-lived misunderstanding at a time of incomplete and evolving scientific knowledge. They point with pride to the Vatican Observatory, founded in the eighteenth century and credited with a number of important astronomic discoveries, as proof that the church embraces and contributes positively to science, including astronomy. And they note a long list of eminent Catholic scientists, from Leonardo da Vinci to Gregor Mendel, the founder of modern genetics, who offer a compelling counter-narrative.

One of the hotly contested issues, partly of historical record and partly of contemporary spin, concerns the extent to which the Protestant Reformers joined the Catholic Church in suppressing heliocentricism—Copernicus in particular. Defenders of Protestantism who view the Reformation as a liberalizing force in Western civilization would prefer a narrative in which the Galileo Affair was solely the province of medieval Christianity. Crassly put, Protestantism scores points over Catholicism if the Reformation fathers behaved better than the Vatican as to heliocentrism. But if the Protestants were as closed-minded and censorial about heliocentricism as the Catholics, then critics of Christianity writ large have a potent argument for the inherent incompatibility of Christianity and science: It will take more than Ninety-Five Theses for the Bible and science to mix.

The historical record is somewhat murky. Many commentators, particularly those critical of orthodox Christianity, have taken the position that Protestants also suppressed Copernicanism. The position that "Protestantism was no less zealous against the new scientific doctrine" than Catholicism was staked by Andrew Dickson White, the first president of Cornell University, in his 1896 *History of the Warfare of Science with Theology in Christendom*, a book that propagated a modernist historical narrative of Christianity versus science.[10] Thomas Kuhn, the eminent philosopher of science (at some point, you may have had to read *The Structure of Scientific Revolutions*), popularized the claim that John Calvin, Martin Luther, and Philip Melanchthon urged the suppression of Copernican ideas and that the Lutherans made life difficult for Copernican scholars at the University of Wittenberg.[11] Indeed, Kuhn argued that Protestantism was, if anything, more hostile to Copernicanism than was Catholicism, since the Protestants "wished to return to a pristine Christianity" based "on the words of Jesus and the early Fathers of the church," which required strict biblical textualism.[12] Kuhn asserts that Protestants were less successful in suppressing Copernicanism only because "they never possessed the police apparatus available to the Catholic church."[13]

These charges seem to be overstated. Although Luther accepted geocentricism, as did most educated people of his day, and he may have made an offhand remark critical of Copernicus (whether he called him "a fool" or just wrong is the subject of some debate), but there is scant evidence that he sought to suppress heliocentricism as a theory. Further, important followers of Luther actively worked to promote Copernicanism. Owen Gingerich, a professor of history of science at the Harvard-Smithsonian Center for Astrophysics, shows that when *De revolutionibus orbium coelestium* was first published in Nuremberg in 1543, the Lutheran bishop Tiedemann Giese demanded the removal of a disclaimer stating that the book was a mathematical device for calculation rather than a genuine description of celestial bodies.[14] Giese wanted a tract to be included in the book and written by a Lutheran scholar, Georg Joachim Rheticus, explaining that the scriptural arguments usually made against heliocentricism were misconceived. Further, Melanchthon, Luther's right-hand man, may have facilitated, rather than suppressed, the exploration of Copernican ideas at the University of Wittenberg, making the university the leading center for the study of Copernicanism in Europe.

Similarly, although Calvin may also have made a fairly casual remark critical of Copernicus, there is no historical evidence showing that he took a firm theological line against it or worked actively to suppress the spread of Copernican science in Geneva or elsewhere. As to both Luther and Calvin, the strongest critical claim that the historical record seems to permit is that they, like most of their educated contemporaries, believed in geocentricism and were personally skeptical of Copernicus.

The fact that an active debate about the Protestant Reformers' interaction with heliocentricism persists shows the continuing symbolic importance of the Galileo Affair. It is too consequential simply to rest in history books as an event from a bygone age. The Galileo Affair seems to abide permanently in a cultural spin room with its meaning and morals up for grabs.

For contemporary Christians, Galileo still offers much to ponder. A concluding thought experiment: Suppose that you wake up tomorrow morning and learn that, overnight, scientists have detected interstellar radio communications that seem to be messages from a civilization on a distant planet. How would you react? Consider the problem from the perspective of your current understanding of the Bible and, if you observe a conflict, would you then insist that the scientists must be wrong? Would you reconsider your theology to make your biblical interpretation fit this new information? Or would you insist that this scientific discovery has no bearing on your theology one way or another, since the Bible and science occupy different spheres?

Galileo's *Dialogue* raised just these sorts of questions. Four hundred years later, they continue to orbit around us.

CHAPTER 3

Voltaire's *Candide*: Enlightenment Rationalism and the Church's Thin Skin

"There is a concatenation of events in this best of all possible worlds: for if you had not been kicked out of a magnificent castle for the love of Miss Cunégonde: if you had not been put into the Inquisition: if you had not walked over America: if you had not stabbed the Baron: if you had not lost all your sheep from the fine country of El Dorado: you would not be here eating preserved citrons and pistachio-nuts."

Final Speech of Dr. Pangloss
Voltaire, *Candide* (1759)

On June 8, 1794, a crowd of thousands of fervent revolutionaries descended on the Tuileries Garden in Paris for the commencement of a brand-new religious holiday—the Festival of the Supreme Being—which had recently been ordained by the Jacobin National Assembly. After political leaders gave speeches, a statute representing atheism was set alight, for Maximilien Robespierre would not have his revolution turned into an atheistic bacchanalia. The French Revolution and the Reign of Terror would be religious . . . in their own way.

Speeches over, the crowd proceeded toward the Champ de Mars, where they found an enormous man-made mountain erected out of timber and plaster, covered with rocks, shrubs, flowers, lights, and mirrors, and topped with a liberty tree. Looming above the mountain, perched on a Doric column, towered the semi-naked marble figure of Hercules. Citizen Robespierre, dressed in a blue overcoat and gold trousers, led the deputies to the mountaintop and then descended from the heights to martial band music. He made two rousing speeches that day, urging the wholehearted worship of an undefined Supreme Being (which somehow seemed to reflect both

"Nature" and the revolutionary spirit of the French people) and chastising priests who "harness us, like vile animals, to the chariots of kings and give to the world examples of baseness, price, perfidy, avarice, debauchery, and falsehood." The rhetorical assault on the clergy went far beyond idle words—the revolution was in the process of purging France of thirty thousand priests through forced abdication and marriage, deportation, or the guillotine.

The Festival of the Supreme Being marked an extraordinary moment of political and religious pageantry that owed much of its inspiration to the philosophical and literary contributions of a man who had died fifteen years earlier, but who had been disinterred and reburied in the Parisian Pantheon in 1791 with full revolutionary honors. On the catafalque bearing his coffin the revolutionaries had written: "He combatted atheists and fanatics. He inspired tolerance. He reclaimed the rights of man against serfdom and feudalism."[1] Inside the coffin lay François-Marie Arouet. We know him simply as Voltaire.

Along with the *philosophes* Jean-Jacques Rousseau and Denis Diderot, Voltaire embodied the eighteenth-century French Enlightenment and its values of rationalism, anti-clerical deism, and rejection of conventional moralism. As much as he would become a divine to the revolution, he was a demon to the church of his day. Among Voltaire's many scandalous writings, one in particular provoked the ire of both the Catholic and Protestant churches. *Candide*, a satirical, ribald little travelogue of a novella that Voltaire published in 1759—largely in reaction to the devastating Lisbon earthquake of 1755 and the German metaphysicist Gottfried Leibniz's philosophy of "optimism"—was banned and burned in both Catholic Paris and Calvinist Geneva. Religious authorities insisted that the book was bad for both morals and religion. Its morals were certainly crude, and its religion irreverent. But what really annoyed the church was that the book poked spiteful fun at various institutions of the church—the Inquisition, Jesuits, missionaries, Anabaptists, and more. The church has never liked being contradicted, but it has especially hated being ridiculed. *Candide* was neither the first nor the last book to get under the church's skin through mockery and derision, but it certainly set the standard for anyone who might try.

THE FIRST INTERNATIONAL CELEBRITY

Voltaire was born in Paris in 1694 during the interminable reign of Louis XIV. He grew up in a prosperous professional family but frequently clashed with his father, a lawyer who was rapidly climbing the social ladder of the *Ancien Régime* (the "old order") that Voltaire would come to despise. Sigmund Freud, whom we shall study in chapter 6, would have been quick to note that Voltaire's first play, *Oedipe*, concerns a man who murders his father.

At the age of ten, Voltaire was shipped off to boarding school for a classical education at the Jesuit College of Paris, an elite training ground still in existence today. Voltaire's father next arranged for the young man to spend some time in the Hague (in the Netherlands), as private secretary to the French ambassador, a sojourn that ended badly when the amorous Voltaire fell madly in love with "Pimpette" (Olympe Dunoyer), a twenty-one-year-old French Huguenot refugee who had already been engaged twice and married once, had borne a child, and had been abandoned by her husband. The ambassador strictly forbade the liaison. Voltaire nonetheless pursued it with the zest of a lovelorn Parisian and ended up shanghaied back to Paris where his father threatened to have him imprisoned. Thus began a lifelong pattern of lusty affairs and reckless insubordination to authority.

Another, and perhaps related, lifelong pattern began shortly thereafter. In 1715, *Oedipe* was introduced in Paris to tremendous acclaim, earning Voltaire a generous annual stipend from the government. But it wasn't long before Voltaire penned an anonymous but quickly recognized poem scurrilously suggesting that the French regent was engaging in incest. The intemperate poet landed in the Bastille for eleven months. Freed at last, Voltaire continued to advance his career as a playwright, living on the fruits of his writing and various shady financial schemes. (On one occasion, for example, Voltaire and some accomplices conspired to corner a national lottery, earning handsome profits in the undertaking.)

As Voltaire grew in reputation as a public intellectual, he seldom found himself lacking both friends and enemies in high places. In 1726, when Voltaire was thirty-two, he was sucked into a feud with a young nobleman—the chevalier de Rohan-Chabot—who had mocked

Voltaire for abandoning his birth name (François-Marie Arouet) and assuming a new one. Voltaire acquired a pair of pistols, took swordsmanship lessons, and challenged him to duel (which was never fought). The Rohan-Chabot family used political connections to have Voltaire thrown again into the Bastille. By playing his own political connections, Voltaire managed to be released into exile in England.

Voltaire's two and a half years in England proved consequential to the development of his intellectual and political views. The Frenchman circulated through London high society, mixing with literary lions such as Alexander Pope and the satirist Jonathan Swift (whose work would inspire Voltaire's own great satire, *Candide*), absorbing the Shakespeare canon, and—most dangerously—obtaining a fondness for the liberal spirit of England's constitutional monarchy, including its broad freedoms of speech and conscience. The ideas he developed in England bore fruit as a collection of essays—*Letters Concerning the English Nation*—that Voltaire published illegally in 1733 after he had returned to Paris. Although ostensibly critical of England, the essays effectively praised the liberality of the English spirit in contrast with the dour backwardness of contemporary France. An admirer of Voltaire described the *Letters* as "the first bomb thrown at the *Ancien Régime*."[2] The *Régime* was not amused. The book was ordered to be burned, and Voltaire once again had to flee from Paris.

Voltaire spent the next sixteen years holed away in a picturesque, but apparently uncomfortable, chateau in Cirey in northeastern France with his new and most famous mistress, Émilie du Châtelet. Émilie was twelve years Voltaire's junior and a married mother of three. There was no secret about her relationship with Voltaire, which her husband—an absent army officer—overtly condoned. Partly to steer clear of hot political topics, and partly driven by Émilie's own intellectual interests in Newtonian physics, Voltaire turned much of his energies during these years to natural science and physics, ultimately publishing a book that introduced Newtonian concepts to laypeople.

It was Voltaire's study in physics that brought him to focus on metaphysical and theological issues that would frame his scandalous book *Candide* years later. Early in the eighteenth century, a quarrel broke out between the English mathematician Isaac Newton and the German mathematician Gottfried Leibniz over which of the two had first discovered calculus. While that reputational dispute dominated the personal relationship between Newton and Leibniz, the principles of physical motion that proceeded from the work of both men captured the interest and admiration of Voltaire and Émilie during their years at Cirey. Leibniz, however, did not stop at the laws of physics; he also developed a comprehensive metaphysics that centered on the nature of God. Since God is beneficent, wrote Leibniz, he created the best possible world. Despite the existence of sin, God's goodness is manifested in the immutable laws of nature and emerges as the ultimate reality of the universe. It was this principle of "theodicy," which Voltaire would dub "optimism" or *candide* (a French word meaning "naive optimism"), that ultimately framed his most famous work. If we may posit a chain of causation, Émilie led Voltaire to Newton and Leibniz on mathematics and motion, Leibniz in turn led Voltaire to metaphysics, and in time, to confront the problem of evil in face of God's goodness.

But Voltaire would not turn his pen against Leibniz until several more twists and turns had passed in his dynamic life. In 1741, his love affair with Madame du Châtelet having waned (and, alas, a new affair with his niece commencing) and Émilie having died, Voltaire decamped to the worldly court of Frederick the Great at Potsdam in Germany to serve as a sort of court intellectual. As with so many of Voltaire's relationships, what began as an affair of mutual, sycophantic admiration ended within two years as Voltaire, mired in a financial scandal and a bitter dispute with an intellectual rival, lost Frederick's favor and decamped in disgrace and under threat of imprisonment.

Banned from Paris by Louis XV, Voltaire moved to an estate near Geneva. He spent the next several years in an edgy relationship with Geneva's Calvinists who tried to ban theatrical productions, a prohibition that Voltaire flaunted as much as possible. He left Geneva in 1753 and spent the next five years living nomadically.

Then a catastrophic event in the Western world sparked Voltaire's revolt against Leibniz's views of God's sovereignty. On November 1, 1755—ironically, All Saints Day—a calamitous earthquake and tsunami struck the Portuguese capital of Lisbon, nearly obliterating the city and killing tens of thousands of residents. Perhaps equally distressing to Enlightenment Europe, the disaster destroyed entire libraries of priceless books and works of art. Voltaire swiftly reacted with a *Poem on the Lisbon Disaster (Or, an Examination of the Axiom "All Is Well")*. In the name of the "child and mother heaped in common wreck, [whose] scattered limbs [lay] beneath the marble shafts," the poem attacked defenders of a good, omnipotent God:

> But how conceive a God supremely good,
> Who heaps his favours on the sons he loves
> Yet scatters evil with as large a hand?[3]

The ghosts of Lisbon still haunted Voltaire when, in 1758, he made his last big geographic move, settling into a chateau at Ferney (now known as Ferney-Voltaire), in eastern France just on the French side of the French-Swiss border, with his niece, Madame Denis. It was there that he published his satirical novel *Candide*, a ribald account of the misadventures of the naïve protagonist, Candide, his philosophical mentor Dr. Pangloss (a stand-in for Leibniz's "optimistic" philosophy), and Candide's erstwhile lover, the unfortunate Cunégonde. As we shall see, more than any other of Voltaire's works, *Candide* provoked a bitter reaction from Christian authorities in Europe, both Catholic and Protestant, and secured Voltaire's legacy as the father of the French Enlightenment.

Voltaire spent his waning years in Ferney, hosting many of Europe's most celebrated men, such as Adam Smith and Sir Edward Gibbon. He also turned his attention to the cause of religious liberty and toleration, managing to secure the posthumous exoneration of French Huguenot merchant, Jean Calas, who had been tortured to death on an accusation of murdering his son to prevent his conversion to Catholicism.

In 1778, Voltaire returned to Paris after twenty-five years of exile. Ill, frail, and aware of his impending death, he nonetheless made some rounds with other celebrities in the city, not neglecting finishing touches on an unusual life, such as allowing Benjamin Franklin to induct him as a Freemason. The Catholic Church made a last-ditch effort to obtain a retraction of Voltaire's anti-Christian writings, demanding that he recant or be refused a burial plot in Paris. To the clergymen surrounding his deathbed and asking him to accept the divinity of Jesus, Voltaire is said to have snapped: "In the name of God, Sir, do not speak to me any more about that man, and let me die in peace."[4] Unrepentant (and, contrary to church propaganda, not demented or dying in fear of hell's torments), Voltaire died in

May 1778. Forbidden a burial in Paris, his friends buried him quietly in the Abbey of Scellières in Champagne.

But Voltaire would have the last laugh on the *Ancien Régime*. After the revolution of 1789, a million Parisians turned out to witness his triumphant reburial in the Pantheon in 1791. Voltaire had come home at last to the City of Light.

Voltaire is sometimes misunderstood to have been an atheist. As we saw in the introduction to this chapter, from the revolutionary accolades he received ("he combatted atheists and fanatics") it is clear that he was not. As late as 1743, Voltaire could still protest in (self-serving) correspondence to the bishop of Mirepoix:

> I am a good citizen and a true Catholic. I say it solely because that is what I have always been at heart. I have not written a single page which does not breathe humanity, and I have written many which are sanctified by religion.[5]

Religious maybe, but a true Catholic he was not. Unlike atheists such as Diderot, Voltaire remained a deist, believing in some sort of generally benevolent God but one far removed from direct involvement in the world. Voltaire rejected divine providence, special revelation, miracles, and man as created in the image of God. Consistent with Robespierre's subsequent attempt to create a French civil religion, Voltaire's religion was naturalistic, moralistic, and anti-orthodox—a socially necessary creation. Voltaire famously claimed that "if God did not exist, it would be necessary to invent him."[6] For better or worse, his life and work became symbols of man's "enlightened" effort to create God in the image of man.

POKING FUN AT OPTIMISM AND THE CHURCH

The story of *Candide* begins in the Westphalian castle of the baron of Thunder-ten-Tronckh, whose ridiculous, overwrought name sets the tone for the ludicrous tale to come. Candide, the bastard son of the baron's sister, is described as a youth of "most gentle manners," "true judgment," and "simplicity of spirit."[7] He loves the beautiful Cunégonde, the baron's daughter. Candide's tutor, Dr. Pangloss, a "professor of metaphysico-theologo-cosmolo-nigology," teaches "that things cannot be otherwise than as they are; for all being created for an end, all is necessarily for the best end" (9). He is, in short, Gottfried Leibniz.

Alas, Candide's bucolic innocence in the castle soon comes crashing down. One day, walking in a park near the castle, Cunégonde chances upon Dr. Pangloss "giving a lesson in experimental natural philosophy" (a tart euphemism) to the chambermaid (10). Ideas planted, Cunégonde makes overtures the next day to Candide, who being discovered by the baron *in delicto flagrante* with his daughter, is run out of the castle "with great kicks on the backside" while Cunégonde faints away (10).

All of this opening is told in a breathless two pages, setting the rapid-fire pace for the rest of the book. In short order, the destitute Candide is impressed into military service by Bulgar soldiers (a wry allusion to the homosexuality of Frederick's Prussian court), flogged, threatened with execution, and forced to witness a brutal battle between "Bulgar and Avar" forces—an ill-disguised allusion to the hostilities between the Prussians and French during the Seven Years' War. Escaping, he decamps to Holland, where he meets mostly hard-hearted people, except for Jacques, an Anabaptist who shows him kindness, thus bolstering Candide's moral optimism. Candide then reencounters Pangloss, now a beggar disfigured by syphilis, who recounts how Cunégonde and her whole family were murdered by the Bulgars. Jacques manages to cure Pangloss of his syphilis, at the cost of an ear and an eye. Despite all of the evil the book's characters have befallen, Pangloss remains Panglossian, insisting that "all this was indispensable . . . for misfortunes make the general good, so that the more private misfortunes there are the greater is the general good" (16).

The terrible sequence that follows reflects Voltaire's earlier lamentation on the Lisbon earthquake and gives *Candide*'s narrative its beating heart. Jacques has business in Lisbon and takes Pangloss and Candide with him by boat. In Lisbon's harbor, a terrible storm buffets the ship. Jacques saves a sailor thrown overboard and is himself thrown overboard in the process. The sailor refuses to help him, and the charitable Jacques tragically drowns. Candide is coming to his aid, but Pangloss stays his hand, explaining that "the Bay of Lisbon had been made on purpose for the purpose of the Anabaptist to be drowned" (16–17). The ship then is dashed to bits, with everyone aboard drowned except for Candide, Pangloss, and the ungrateful sailor, who make it to the shore. No sooner have the survivors gotten their bearings in the Portuguese capital than the calamitous earthquake hits, wounding Candide. Candide begins to despair, but Pangloss consoles him with the knowledge that "it is impossible for things to be other than they are; for everything is right" (18). This comment is overheard by an Inquisitor who takes Pangloss's optimism as heretical in light of the doctrine of original sin. Pangloss and Candide are arrested by the Inquisition and subjected to an auto-da-fé—translated as "act of faith," but in reality torture and execution by burning at the stake—to atone for the earthquake, along with a few other randomly selected citizens. Pangloss is hanged (spoiler alert: he's not really dead) and Candide brutally whipped. (As with most events in *Candide*, this one wasn't invented; the Portuguese Inquisition in fact conducted a similar auto-da-fé on June 20, 1756). Candide escapes the clutches of the Inquisition when a second earthquake strikes Lisbon and flees lamenting for himself, Pangloss, the Anabaptist, and Cunégonde. Doubts are beginning to form about Pangloss's philosophy: "If this is the best of possible worlds, then what are the others?" (19).

To borrow an expression from Kurt Vonnegut, and "so it goes" for the rest of the story. In short order, Candide reencounters his beloved Cunégonde, who had in fact been raped and disemboweled by the Bulgars, but somehow survived and now lives in sexual slavery to a Grand Inquisitor and a Jew who share her time and body. Candide kills her two captors and escapes to South America with Cunégonde and a similarly unfortunate old woman. In the New World, Candide races through a series of adventures and misadventures, losing Cunégonde to other suitors, meeting and then murdering her Jesuit brother (or so it seems), nearly being eaten by anti-Jesuit cannibals, and making and then losing a fortune from the mythical city of El Dorado. Eventually, Candide makes his way back to Europe in the company of Martin, a Manichean scholar who stands in for Leibniz's real-life philosophical antagonist, the French Protestant scholar Pierre Bayle. Despite all of the woes he has encountered, Candide clings to his optimism. His sanguine attitude persists even after the party arrives in England and observes an admiral shot for not killing enough of the enemy (an allusion to Royal Navy officer John Byng, who was shot in 1757 for allowing Minorca to fall to the French). He also finally catches up with Cunégonde, who has become horribly ugly due to her misfortunes. On a happier note, Candide stumbles across Pangloss and Cunégonde's brother, who both somehow escaped death only to be sold as rowing slaves on a ship. Candide buys their freedom and then marries Cunégonde, despite her horrid appearance and his lack of desire to marry his childhood sweetheart, only to spite her Jesuit brother who continues to prohibit the marriage.

The book ends on less frenetic note as Candide and his entourage retire to a country farm. He receives a final bit of advice from a Turkish philosopher, who encourages him to devote his life to simple things and to avoid further external entanglements. Pangloss attempts to reinvigorate Candide's optimism, pointing out that the whole preceding train of events was necessary to his present bucolic happiness. Candide finally dismisses his old mentor's philosophizing, accepting the Turk's advice and insisting, "Let us cultivate our garden" (81).

For understandable reasons, Voltaire signed *Candide* with a pseudonym ("Dr. Ralph") and initially denied authorship, insisting that "people must have lost their senses to attribute to me that pack of nonsense." However, as the eminent historian Will Durant observed:

> But France was unanimous: no other man could have written *Candide*. Here was that deceptively simple, smoothly flowing, lightly prancing, impishly ironic prose that only he could write; here and there a little obscenity, a little scatology; everywhere a playful, darting, lethal irreverence; if the style is the man, this had to be Voltaire.[8]

Candide was quickly recognized not only as Voltaire's handiwork but also as an important literary achievement. Literary critic Elie Fréron, Voltaire's literary archenemy, may have opined that *Candide* was an overly dark and pessimistic book that "first arouses the mind, but eventually strikes despair into the heart,"[9] but its popular reception was overwhelmingly positive. As Voltaire's biographer Ian Davidson wrote:

> It is easy to see why *Candide* was so popular with ordinary readers and so unpopular with the authorities. It is a highly entertaining little tale, at once so pessimistic and so gay, which through the medium of a knowingly unrealistic and picturesque international travel adventure, makes skeptical fun of the theologians, metaphysicians, Jesuits, and inquisitors.[10]

Candide had struck the public's fancy, and it had also struck a nerve with the church.

CENSORSHIP

Hardly had *Candide* hit the presses when church and state leaped into action to suppress it. In Paris, Advocate-General Omer Joly de Fleury declared it "contrary to religion and morals," the city council banned the book, and the French police began an operation to seize and destroy all copies. In 1762, *Candide* joined Galileo's *Dialogue* on the Inquisition's *Index Librorum Prohibitorum*, adding the official sanction of the Vatican to that of the civil authorities of Paris.

The censorial reaction, however, wasn't limited to Catholic authorities. The Calvinist Genevan pastors also denounced Candide as "full of dangerous principles concerning religion and tending to moral depravation,"[11] and the Grand Council of Geneva banned it. To add insult to injury, the Grand Council then banned citizens of Geneva from performing in Voltaire's theater.

Nor did the controversy around *Candide* die out with the advent of modernity. As late as 1929, an American customs official in Boston denied a number of copies of *Candide* from reaching a French class at Harvard University, labeling the book as obscene.[12] That decision was widely ridiculed and soon reversed, but it accentuated the staying power of the suspicion that Voltaire's magnum opus should never be read by decent people.

The censorship campaign wasn't successful and, indeed, may have contributed to surging demand for the book. (See chapter 1 on the "forbidden fruits" effect.) By the end of 1759, no fewer than seventeen different French language editions had appeared in the Francophone world, not to mention an additional three English-language editions published in London and an Italian edition. Within a year, the book had sold between twenty and thirty thousand copies, making it a runaway best-seller for its day. Over time, *Candide* has been translated into scores of languages, read by millions of readers from bored schoolchildren to curious adults, and crowned the leading light of the French Enlightenment and one of the most significant works of all time. The last laugh was Voltaire's, but the church never managed to find it funny.

WHY THE CHURCH DIDN'T FIND IT FUNNY

Voltaire did not write *Candide* with a view to making new friends in the church. Along its ribald path, the book managed to insult the Inquisition, Jesuits, missionaries, the Catholic Church more generally, and even a variety of Protestants. The book's satirical take on Christianity reached beyond the intellectual elite and took hold in popular culture. The expression "Let's eat a Jesuit" became a common punch line in France.

Still, one may ask why this particular work in Voltaire's canon became the focal point for such a strong reaction by the church. Voltaire had experienced a variety of forms of censorship of works that affronted the church or state. For example, his 1741 play *Mahomet*, which mocked the Muslim religion but was also perceived as undermining all revealed religion, including Catholicism, was forced off the stage in Lille after only three performances. But Voltaire had never experienced a reaction so vehement as the attack on *Candide*. Why? There are certainly prurient passages in *Candide*, and the book throws barbed critiques at prevailing theological orthodoxy, but Voltaire had already written everything theologically provocative about divine sovereignty and the problem of evil in his earlier poem on the Lisbon earthquake. He had also written bawdy works earlier, as in his *Jeanne la Pucelle*, which mocked hagiographic accounts of Joan of Arc by imagining the maid of Orleans constantly pursued by lustful monks and soldiers. A decade earlier, he had written *Zadig*, a story with a plotline similar to *Candide* involving a character at the whim of Fate evidencing a world of arbitrary fortune, and *Sermon de cinquante*, which scathingly attacked the Christian religion. *Candide* does not apparently seem to rank above these other works on the theological or prurience offense scale.

The answer, however, seems to be that church could stand many provocations but not being mocked and ridiculed. *Candide* did not merely narrate scenes that might appeal to prurient interest or advance ideas that might cause people to question the church. It had people openly *laughing at the church*. The church is made not merely to look wrong; it is made to look ludicrous.

To contemplate the biting power of satire, think back on times in your own life when someone has said something about you that left you especially hurt or angry. Perhaps you will discover that many of the most hurtful or infuriating episodes involved mockery or ridicule. Imagine that someone says, "You're ugly." That will sting. But now imagine that someone starts pretending that you're beautiful in order to suggest that you're actually just the opposite. That stings even more.

In 1971, leftist activist Saul Alinsky published his final book, *Rules for Radicals: A Practical Primer for Realistic Radicals*, summing up his life-learned lessons for how relatively powerless people can most effectively agitate for social change. Here is Alinsky's fifth rule: "Ridicule is man's most potent weapon. It's hard to counterattack ridicule, and it infuriates the opposition, which then reacts to your advantage."[13] Alinsky is onto something, and his insight resonates with the story of *Candide* and the church. So long as Voltaire was advancing rational arguments—even vehement ones—against the Christian faith, the church could respond in equal measure. But how could the church respond to a book that purported to advance the view that God is good and sovereign, all the while making that position look more and more ludicrous through cheeky storytelling? How, for example, could one give credence to Pangloss's continued optimism after all the terrible (and, frankly, ridiculous) things that befell Candide's merry band of friends? What arguably most upset the church about *Candide* is that it was, to quote Alinsky, "hard to counterattack the ridicule." This is why the church devoted so much effort to having the book destroyed and then, when at last Voltaire's dying body fell into their hands, worked cruelly to exact the author's retraction of his own mockery.

There is a further, gloomier, perspective that needs to be expressed about the church's reaction to *Candide*. Voltaire was not just mocking Christianity or the church in the abstract. He was mocking specific, contemporaneous institutions of Christianity: (the Inquisition, Jesuits, New World missionaries, and Anabaptists.) Personal honor, reputation, and pride were at stake. Is it possible that at least some of the church's ire against *Candide* had less to do with "dangerous principles concerning religion" and more to do with "dangerous principles concerning *us*"?

It is human nature to associate our own egos, pride, and honor with greater causes. The church can never be too zealous for the honor of God and his word, but it can take *itself* too seriously. All too often, Christian institutions and individuals have conflated their own honor with the Lord's. When artist Andres Serrano displayed a crucifix submerged in urine in an NEA-funded exhibit, I was offended *for Christ*—and I hope that you were too. When a comedian mocks American evangelicals, we may feel annoyed, but I hope that we will not conflate our annoyance at the insult to us personally with an insult to Christ and the gospel. (Yes, we are called to be Christ's ambassadors in the world, but not all criticisms of us are undeserved or, even indirectly, bring dishonor to Christ.)

How, then, should Christians think about works of satire that tend to mock and ridicule? On the one hand, the Scriptures are full of accounts of Christians coming under ridicule. When the young men of Bethel mocked Elisha's baldness, God sent two bears to teach them a lesson (2 Kings 2:23–24). And, of course, it was not enough that the Roman soldiers beat and crucified Jesus and cast lots for his garments; they had to dress him in purple and bow down in mock worship (Mark 15:17). Then again, at times biblical heroes have resorted to mocking God's enemies as well. When the prophets of Baal were unable to bring down fire to consume the altar, Elijah mocked them loudly, suggesting that perhaps Baal had taken a journey or was sleeping (1 Kings 18:27). And the apostle Paul had choice words for agitators insisting that gentile Christians observe all Jewish customs, suggesting that they "go the whole way and emasculate themselves" (Gal. 5:12).

Satire poses unique challenges for Christians, who are called to love their enemies (Matt. 5:44), turn the other cheek (Matt. 5:39), engage in speech seasoned with salt (Col. 4:6), and speak the truth in love (Eph. 4:15). Not being a Christian, however, Voltaire operated under no such constraint. He exerted the full force of his considerable intellect and writer's craft to debase and humiliate his foes. *Candide* is not a gracious book, nor one that pokes gentle fun or invites everyone to share the joke. It hits its targets ferociously and with malice. And it often stoops to juvenile crude humor. Nonetheless, it is a great book—great in the sense of having stoked the popular imagination about real problems in society and in the church, about hypocrisy, theological absurdities, and grave injustices. At first, the church didn't want to hear Voltaire's message. Eventually, it had no choice.

CANDIDE'S CONTINUING TRAVELS

As a book, *Candide* has enjoyed a marvelous career. It is widely considered one of the finest satires in the canon of Western literature, has been translated into many languages, and read by millions of readers. "Panglossian"—meaning "excessively optimistic"—has now become a common adjective in the English language. The book has been credited with influencing subsequent literary genres, such as dystopian science fiction (think Aldous Huxley's *Brave New World* and George Orwell's *1984*). *Candide* even made it to the big stage, opening as a Leonard Bernstein Broadway operetta in 1956 (alas, it flopped when it first opened but it is still going strong today).

Candide's scathing critique of excessive optimism has also grown with time. Writing after the horrors of World War I, Aldous Huxley observed that *Candide*'s pessimism has "become the everyday wisdom of all the world since 1914."[14] That, of course, was before the horrors of World War II and the genocides, atrocities, and calamities of the later twentieth century and beyond. The Lisbon earthquake was horrific enough—but imagine what Voltaire's quill would have done with the Holocaust, the Great Chinese Famine, the specter of nuclear war, or the AIDS epidemic. For skeptics of God's providential sovereignty and goodness, the themes raised by *Candide* have seemingly found ever increasing evidence.

The church has not been immune to these sufferings, nor to the cry of the prophet Habakkuk to a God who at times seems inattentive to suffering and injustice. Nor has the church been unable to mount a thoughtful response to the questions Voltaire so poignantly raised in *Candide*. In *The Problem of Pain*, C. S. Lewis tackled Voltaire's question directly, posing it in the form of dilemma:

> If God were good, He would make His creatures perfectly happy, and if He were almighty He would be able to do what he wished. But the creatures are not happy. Therefore God lacks either goodness, or power, or both.[15]

Acknowledging the limitations on finite man's ability to account for the judgment of an infinite God, Lewis nonetheless offers some compelling ways to understand the reasons why a good, loving, and omnipotent God might nevertheless allow pain in the world. Of course, neither Voltaire nor Lewis was the first or last authority on these questions. They are age-old, as old as the book of Job, and ones we will make out in this life, at best, through a glass darkly.

If we are looking, ironically, for some optimism coming out of *Candide*, perhaps we can find it in the spirit of enlightenment and toleration that Voltaire and his philosophe contemporaries tried to kindle in Europe. Perhaps the experience of *Candide*—of the church's reactionary suppression of a book that threatened its dignity—has at least taught us to be more tolerant of works that make us feel uncomfortable. Perhaps, at a minimum, we can concur with Voltaire in his *Treatise on Toleration* (1763) that "every citizen [should] be free to follow his own reason, and believe whatever this enlightened or deluded reason shall dictate to him."[16] Maybe Voltaire at least managed to kindle a spirit of toleration, openness, and dialogue that permits contending viewpoints to coexist without violence on the public stage.

Alas (and furthering Voltaire's case for pessimism), we are unable to claim even that modest moral victory from the *Candide* affair. Ironically, the revolutionaries who so honored Voltaire didn't particularly share his spirit of toleration for offending books or ideas. During the Reign of Terror that began in 1793, "in Paris alone, more than 8,000 books were destroyed; elsewhere, more than 4 million, of which 26,000 were ancient manuscripts."[17] Venezuelan scholar Fernando Báez notes that "it was a bad time for books. When wasn't it?"[18] Many contemporary Christians experiencing the changing tides of popular culture and political correctness may relate to this historical irony. Increasingly, it seems that those who have long accused the church of intolerance are agitating for restrictions on the rights of Christians to profess and live their faith—for example, in the deployment of anti-discrimination laws against people adhering to traditional Christian views. There is no longer any question of whether *Candide* will be tolerated; there does, however, seem to be a question of whether the church will be.

But perhaps the greatest threat to the church is a different one—a subtle temptation whispered at the very end of Voltaire's magnum opus. Maybe the most invidious aspect of *Candide* is not its bold attack on theodicy, but the moral of its closing lines. As we saw, the character

Candide ends his namesake novella with the assertion "But we must cultivate our garden," an aphorism urging that we focus on simple activities in our immediate environment rather than globetrotting in search of grand pretentions. For many Christians, the phenomena Voltaire described—widespread suffering and evil and the seemingly unanswerable challenges they pose for orthodox Christianity—are reasons to do just what Voltaire suggested: lead a quiet, pious life minding one's own business, keeping one's head down, staying out of trouble, and avoiding rocking the boat.

Such temptations to isolation and localism—to cultivate our gardens—may be Voltaire's enlightened wisdom, but they are not from God. Although Christians are admonished to lead quiet lives and work with their hands in order to win the respect of others (1 Thess. 4:9–12), Jesus commanded his disciples *not* to stay at home cultivating their gardens, but rather to go into the whole world and spread the good news of his kingdom (Mark 16:15). And Paul told Timothy that we haven't been given a spirit of timidity, but a spirit of power (2 Tim. 1:7). Without becoming the insipid Dr. Pangloss, the church must boldly and fearlessly confront the evil in the world, assured that in this and in all things, we are more than conquerors (Rom. 8:37).

In *Candide*, Voltaire threw down the gauntlet to the church. The church responded by trying to bury it six feet under. That didn't work. The gauntlet is still lying there. We have no choice but to pick it up.

CHAPTER 4

Charles Darwin's *Origin of Species*: The Many Faces of Evolutionary Theory

"I see no good reason why the views given in this volume should shock the religious feelings of anyone."

Charles Darwin
The Origin of Species (1859)

In the scorching heat of a midsummer Tennessee afternoon, the two titanic orators of their day, William Jennings Bryan and Clarence Darrow, met on the only battlefield appropriate to their station—the courthouse. Actually, the operatic encounter took place just outside the courthouse on an elevated platform where the trial had moved to accommodate the thousands of spectators and reporters who had flocked to witness the most theatrical trial in American history. It was the "Scopes Monkey Trial," a staged criminal prosecution of a young Tennessee schoolteacher for teaching Charles Darwin's theories of evolution. Darrow, the greatest criminal defense lawyer of his generation, represented the accused and, in a surreal turn of events, was cross-examining William Jennings Bryan, the deeply religious former secretary of state and Democratic presidential nominee known as the "Great Commoner," who also led the prosecution team.

The trial arose from a newly minted Tennessee statute, passed in early 1925, making it illegal to teach that man had descended from another life form. Even in a thoroughly religious and conservative state such as Tennessee, the statute was slated to fail in the Legislature until the showman-evangelist Billy Sunday held eighteen days of revival meetings in Memphis, reaching an audience of two hundred thousand. Kicking, sweating, and sliding across the stage, Sunday proclaimed evolutionary theory flatly contrary to the Bible: "I don't believe the old bastard theory of evolution. . . . I believe I am just as God Almighty made me."[1] Confronted with a popular swell of anti-evolutionary religious fervor, the Tennessee legislature quickly passed the statute.

Shortly after the passage of the new law, civic leaders in Dayton, Tennessee, saw an opportunity to put their city on the map and generate revenue by staging a trial pitting religion against science. The scheme succeeded beyond their wildest dreams. The city fathers found a young schoolteacher, John Scopes, willing to become the scapegoat and procured a prosecution against him for teaching evolution in the public schools. One thing quickly led to another and, by July, Scopes was on trial in Dayton. Darrow—standing in for skepticism, science, and modernity—acted as Scopes's chief lawyer, and Bryan—standing in for faith, religion, and tradition—his chief antagonist.

By the time Bryan sensationally took the stand, the whole affair had swelled into an international drama covered by two hundred reporters from around the world and broadcast live on WGN radio station. Dayton morphed into a Ringling Brothers production, with trained chimps performing on the courthouse lawn, itinerant evangelists roaming the streets proclaiming fire and brimstone on evolution, and hucksters selling monkey mementos to cash in on what *Time Magazine* called "the fantastic cross between a circus and a holy war."[2] That Darrow took the unprecedented step of calling the lead opposing lawyer as a witness—and that Bryan accepted—fueled the trial's waning moments into an event that even Hollywood could not outsensationalize when it finally told the story in 1960 in *Inherit the Wind*.

Darrow and Bryan met for hand-to-hand combat on the seventh and penultimate day of trial. The *New York Times* described the encounter as "the most amazing courtroom scene in Anglo-American history."[3] Ditching any pretense that the trial concerned the legal guilt or innocence of John Scopes, Darrow and Bryan gave the watching world what it wanted: a no-holds barred debate on science versus the Bible.

Was Jonah really swallowed by a whale? asked Darrow. Yes, "a big fish, and I believe it, and I believe in a God who can make a whale and make a man and make both do what he pleases," retorted Bryan, bringing the matter pointedly back to evolution. Did Joshua actually command the sun to stand still? Certainly. Did Noah's flood actually destroy the earth six thousand years ago? Yes. Whom did Cain marry? Bryan couldn't exactly say.

As the cross-examination progressed, Darrow surged and Bryan slumped. Pressed on the details of how miraculous events recorded in the Bible could have happened, Bryan repeatedly had to admit that he did not know. Darrow refused to take ignorance for an answer, pressing Bryan to hazard guesses. When Bryan admitted that he did not know how to calculate the Great Flood's date at 4004 BC, Darrow demanded that Bryan provide some sort of account: "What do you think?"

Testily, Bryan snapped: "I do not think about things I don't think about."

With a trial lawyer's deadly feel for the jugular, Darrow shot back, "Do you think about things you do think about?"

Bryan's response reflected the world-weariness of an old man who knew he was beaten: "Well, sometimes."

The trial transcript records that laughter rang out in the courtyard. The historical transcript records that laughter rang out around the world. Bryan was surely no slouch in the world of hard-nosed verbal jousting. His silver-tongued "Cross of Gold" speech denouncing the gold standard at the 1896 Democratic National Convention ranks among the greatest political speeches in American history. But Darrow's outfoxing of Bryan on that July day in 1925 seemed to encapsulate for the world the final, ignorant, know-nothing futility of the fundamentalist revolt against Darwinism. And, then, as if to play out the moment's pageantry to perfection, three days later Bryan died of apoplexy, or perhaps a broken heart. The satirical journalist H. L. Mencken, who covered the trial with a vicious wit, ungraciously memorialized Bryan as "one of the most tragic asses in American history,"[4] a man whose struggle and death in Dayton pantomimed the struggle and inevitable demise of religious fundamentalism itself.

The Scopes Monkey Trial did not end the church's confrontation with Darwinism, but it did popularly crystallize the view that religious objection to evolutionary theory was demonstrably ignorant and backwards; and, further, that if the church was so wrong about evolution, then it must be wrong about many other things as well. That, after all, was the real point of Darrow's cross-examination, and it has proved a sneer most difficult to shake.

How did it come to this? The story begins in Plymouth harbor, England, in 1831 with the extraordinary voyage of a curious young

naturalist aboard the Royal Navy's brig-sloop *HMS Beagle*. The book
that Charles Darwin published nearly thirty years later drawing on
insights from his days on the *Beagle*—*The Origin of Species*—would
set in a motion a scientific, philosophical, and moral revolution that
would rock the church like an earthquake.

CHARLES DARWIN ON AND OFF THE *BEAGLE*

Charles Darwin (1809–82) did not set out to rock the church.
Indeed, he almost did not set out on the *Beagle* at all. Darwin's father,
a wealthy capitalist, from Shropshire, England, forbade him to go on
the voyage, thinking it a waste of time, and he only relented when
Darwin's uncle intervened. The *Beagle*'s captain, Robert FitzRoy, also
nearly sank twenty-two-year-old Darwin's chances at the life-changing
voyage. FitzRoy, a strong believer in phrenology—extrapolating predictions about character and mental ability from the shape of a person's head—doubted whether someone with Darwin's nose could
possess sufficient energy and determination for the voyage.[5] Nonetheless, through Divine Providence or random luck, on December
7, 1831, Darwin set off on the voyage of the *Beagle* with the goal of
studying nature in far-flung reaches of the globe.

Over the next fifty-seven months, the *Beagle* would circumnavi-
gate the globe, with the predominance of its time spent along the
coasts of South America. The ship's trajectory skirted the west coast of
Africa before sailing across the Atlantic to Brazil. It then crept south
along the east coast of South America with several port calls, before
arriving at Montevideo in Uruguay in July 1832. There Darwin would
disembark and proceed overland via vast swaths of the South American interior—Patagonia and Tierra del Fuego—rendezvousing periodically with the *Beagle*, before the ship finally departed the South
American continent from Valparaiso, Chile, nearly three years later.

Darwin's years on foot and horseback in South America were
filled with harrowing adventure: dangerous encounters with hostile
armies and native tribes; attacks from parasitic, disease-carrying bugs;
treks across the Andes; and surviving the aftermath of a devastating
earthquake in Chile. For a naturalist, however, the greatest adventure
was the opportunity to study the geology and biology of this strange

new continent. An avid shooter, Darwin collected large numbers of animal specimens and carefully catalogued their morphology.

Darwin also carefully studied the varieties in another living species—humans—that he encountered in his journeys. In particular, Darwin was struck with the primitive crudeness of the native people of Tierra del Fuego, people who struck Darwin as almost inhuman. They were, to his eye, almost as close to nonhuman primates as they were to humans. Put aside the use of language, Darwin wrote in his private notebook, and "compare, the Fuegian & Orangutan, & dare to say difference so great."[6] Seeing primitive humans so far from the civilized European ideal led Darwin to doubt the prevailing view of man as a special, non-animal creation. Gradually, Darwin began to shake the traditional creationist views in which he had been acculturated and think provocatively outside the box.

But nothing quite compared to the impression made on Darwin by his month-long stay in 1835 on the Galápagos Islands off the coast of Ecuador, as the *Beagle* left South America and began its circuitous trip back homeward. The Galápagos formed, Darwin later wrote, "a little world within itself," a primeval sphere that brought Darwin nearer than ever to "that mystery of mysteries—the first appearance of new beings on this earth."[7] Here, Darwin encountered a rich variety of unique plant and animal species: seagoing iguanas; red-footed boobies; exquisite cacti; enormous tortoises; and, as he famously reported in later years, distinctive varieties of finches on different islands, each adapted in size to the precise environment of its respective island. All of these species, ridiculously idiosyncratic and yet perfectly adapted to their environments, set the wheels turning in Darwin's young mind. How had these diverse plants and animals come to be in this place? Although he had not yet fully put together the theory of origins that would later become synonymous with his name, the Galápagos Islands imprinted in his mind ideas and understandings that would ultimately inspire and underlie his earthshaking theories.

Departing South America, the *Beagle* completed its circumnavigation of the globe, sailing west across the Pacific with stops in Tahiti, New Zealand, and Australia before rounding the Cape of Good Hope, traversing the southern Atlantic back to the eastern coast of South America, and finally re-traversing the northern Atlantic back to

England. Darwin arrived in England having moved five years ahead in age and leapt decades ahead in his thinking.

Of everything he witnessed during his five long years away, nothing contributed more to his dawning rejection of traditional religious accounts of origins than the differences between species in different locations around the globe. In Darwin's view, if an omnipotent God had created the separate species and assigned them habitats, then he would have spread the same kind of species in different locations with similar climates and living conditions. However, when Darwin surveyed the species in two islands with similar physical ecology—the Cape Verde Islands off Western Africa and the Galápagos Islands off the west coast of South America—he found enormous differences, even though each species closely resembled the species on the nearby continents. It seemed unlikely, wrote Darwin in private correspondence, that "it pleased the Creator . . . that the inhabitants of the Galápagos Archipelago should be related to those of Chile . . . and that all its inhabitants should be totally unlike those of the similarly volcanic and arid Cape Verde and Canary Islands."[8] Something other than divine design must be at work in rendering the plant and animal species of the world.

The "something," of course, was the theory of evolution through natural selection that Darwin proclaimed two decades later in *Origin of Species*. Why did it take Darwin so long to publish his provocative and groundbreaking theory? We know from Darwin's notes and correspondence that he began working out the theory of evolution through natural selection almost immediately upon his arrival back in England, where he soon married and settled down to a life of study that his family wealth could afford him. So the explanation cannot be that he did not come up with the theory until years later. A conventional account holds that Darwin waited to publish his theory because he knew that it would offend the religious and cultural establishment, not to mention his religiously devout wife Emma. While some scholars have disputed this account, there can be no doubt that any religious scruples Darwin might have felt as a young man about publishing his account faded over time.

Born into a conventionally religious family, Darwin at one point had considered entering the priesthood, albeit because such a position would have given him ample time to pursue his passion for natural history. Over the course of many years, however, Darwin drifted toward agnosticism. Some of this drift was intellectual, driven by Darwin's scientific work where a Creator God became first superfluous and then positively a hindrance to his scientific theories. But, as is almost always true in matters of faith and skepticism, much of the drift was intensely personal and circumstantial, driven by the heart rather than the mind. Darwin's worsening physical health made some contribution, but the death of his beloved ten-year-old daughter Annie in 1851 probably contributed to this more than anything else.[9]

Darwin was still dithering over his notes and incomplete drafts on evolution when an extraordinary coincidence sent him scurrying to get a book ready for the presses. In June 1858, Darwin received a manuscript from another well-known British naturalist, Alfred Russel Wallace, sent to Darwin for his comments. To Darwin's chagrin, Wallace's manuscript outlined a theory of evolution through natural selection closely similar to Darwin's own emerging theory. Although the details of the argument differed in some important ways from his own, Darwin immediately saw that if he delayed publication of his own work, people would think he was parroting Wallace. Darwin scrambled to complete a manuscript. A year later, he published his revolutionary book, *On the Origin of Species by Means of Natural Selection or the Preservation of Favoured Races in the Struggle for Life.*

DARWIN'S RADICAL CLAIM: EVOLUTION THROUGH NATURAL SELECTION

Charles Darwin didn't invent the theory of evolution. As far back as Greek antiquity, philosophers such as Anaximander of Miletus (c. 610–546 BC) and Empedocles (ca. 495–435 BC) had argued that plant and animal species descended from other animal species. Philosophers such as Plato and Aristotle with a greater influence on the later Christian tradition argued, to the contrary, that species were fixed in ideal forms reflecting the archetypes or hidden forms of creation. During the medieval period, Christian scholastic thinkers, including Thomas Aquinas, embraced the idealism of Plato and Aristotle, and they organized all living things into a great chain of being, where each creature's place was fixed in a hierarchy from God on down—as we saw with respect to the Galileo Affair in chapter 2.

This hierarchical perspective froze out the possibility of evolution, but with the renewed opportunities for critical inquiry occasioned by the Renaissance and Enlightenment came new forays into evolutionary theory. Naturalists exploring the fossil record found discontinuities between present species and similar, older species, raising the question of what processes caused species to change over time. In 1796, the French naturalist and zoologist Georges Cuvier published his findings that present-day elephants formed a separate species from related predecessor animals such as mammoths and mastodons. Cuvier denied that these inter-special variations evidenced evolution, arguing instead for a cycle of catastrophic destruction and recreation of new species. Other contemporary naturalists, such as Charles Lyell, argued against catastrophism based on a careful study of the earth's geology, which showed evidence of gradual change over long time periods, but also cast doubt on evolution among living species. In 1809, Jean-Baptiste Lamarck argued for the transmutation of species through inherited adaptation. "Lamarckism" became associated with the belief that an animal could change its anatomy in response to its physical environment and then pass on those changes to its offspring.

Darwin was well aware of these sharp controversies in scientific thought about the incidence and nature of change in the natural world. But he was particularly influenced by Thomas Malthus, a thinker who was not a naturalist but who offered a poignant and controversial perspective on life as a form of competition for survival. In 1798, Malthus, an English cleric, published his *Essay on the Principle of Population* portraying population growth as a catastrophic process leading to destruction through famine or disease. Malthus's competitive struggle for existence, in which weaker members of society would be weeded out and the strong would survive, inspired Darwin to name his eventual theory "natural selection."

Evolutionary theory didn't spring full-blown from Darwin's head like Athena from Zeus, but Darwin's famous book made a breakthrough for the theory by offering—in fairly accessible and nontechnical prose—a comprehensive, empirically founded account of how species could transmutate over time. The aim of the book was not to counter religious ideas per se, but rather to advance two separate, but interrelated, ideas: first, that species had not been separately created;

and, second, that natural selection accounted for the development of species over time.

Origin began with a subject that would appeal to readers' common experience—variation of species under domestication. Everyone could see immense differences among the varieties of plant and animal species that man had domesticated. The differences between these domesticated species—horses, dogs, pigeons, hybrid plants—were far greater than the differences between varieties of the same species within nature. This variability, Darwin wrote, "is due to our domestic productions having been raised under conditions of life not so uniform as, and somewhat different from, those to which the parent species had been exposed under nature."[10] Darwin thus established the nonthreatening proposition that husbandry could produce dramatic variation in species—toy poodles hardly recognizable as belonging to the same species as working mastiffs—and that environmental differences contributed to the differences.

Darwin then extended this observation to the natural world. Significant differences could be observed within undomesticated species as well. The differences tended to be greatest among common and widely dispersed species, suggesting that differences in environment led to differences in species. This was a critical step in the argument, because it tended to show that nature conditioned species rather than species finding their proper place in hospitable natural environments, as might occur under creation.

Now Darwin was ready to spring his theory of natural selection. Hearkening back to Malthus, Darwin noted that species would tend to multiply exponentially until they filled up the world unless checked by some counteraction. The obvious counteraction to overexpansion was competition among and within species for resources, which creates a "struggle for existence." Particularly important in Darwin's account was competition within species. Intra-species competition was a ruthless, zero-sum game because all of the animals within a species were naturally vying for the same resources and any slight advantages could determine which varieties thrived or perished. Darwin noted:

> Owing to this struggle, variations, however slight and from whatever cause proceeding, if they be in any degree profitable to the individuals of a species, in their infinitely complex relations to other organic

> beings and to their conditions of life, will tend to the preservation of
> such individuals, and will be generally inherited by the offspring. (75)

Nature thus "selected" for survival those varieties within a species that held some physical advantage over their peers. When a new variation randomly appeared in a plant or an animal, it would either tend to advantage the animal or disadvantage it. The advantageous variations would allow the owner to win the cutthroat game of life or death. The offspring of that owner would then inherit their parents' advantageous quirks, and the entire species would, over time, consist of organisms bearing that trait.

Darwin then added an additional form of selection—sexual selection—that reinforced the transmutation caused by natural selection. Animals tend to propagate their own lineage when they select mates with attractive, survival-enhancing traits, such as horns on a stag or spurs on a rooster. Thus, over many rounds of reproduction, advantageous variations that enter the species will find themselves propagated. All of this happens unconsciously, Darwin argued, through the invisible hand of nature. Animals don't have to know that they are selecting mates with advantageous traits. It just has to be the case that animals that do select mates with advantageous traits see their own variations propagated over time, which creates a selective advantage for animals good at selecting trait-advantaged mates.

In Darwin's view, the combined effects of natural selection and sexual selection added up to an evolutionary process that resembled a great tree of life—the metaphor that has stuck with schoolchildren ever since. Earlier parent species branched out into a variety of offshoot species, each filling its own ecological niche until it too evolved into a variety of new species. Consistent with Lyell's gradualist theories on geologic change, Darwin argued that this process takes place gradually, in tiny increments, over vast periods of time.

Perhaps anticipating the backlash to his theories that would arise in both scientific and religious circles, Darwin spent a good deal of *Origin* anticipating objections to his theory of evolution through natural selection. Of all the objections Darwin preemptively answered, two stand out because of their later salience in debates over evolutionary theory. One major objection that Darwin sought to dispel concerned difficulties in understanding how highly complex traits—

such as eyes or wings—could arise from slight incremental changes. Take the eye, for example. Darwin acknowledged that to think that an organ as incredibly complex as the eye could evolve from a sequence of miniscule random variations seemed, at first blush, "absurd in the highest degree." But, Darwin reasoned, the only necessary condition for evolution in innumerable slight degrees from a "simple and imperfect eye" to the highly complex and adapted eyes of contemporary organisms was that each variation "be useful to any animal under changing conditions of life" (171). Thus if an animal's nerve became slightly photosensitive through random variation and that gave that animal even a slight evolutionary advantage, and any subsequent improvements in the nerve also gave the successor animal a selective advantage, there was no reason that, over a long period of time, the photosensitive nerve couldn't morph into a dazzlingly complicated eye.

The second major objection to his theory that Darwin sought to preempt concerned the ostensible lack of a fossil record evidencing gradual transformations of species. In the fossil record as it stood in Victorian times, species seemed to appear out of nowhere, without ancestors. Darwin answered this "missing link" objection by noting that the existing paleontological record was still sporadic and poor, suggesting that future exploration and discovery might yield new fossils that would show proof of his theories more clearly. But he also cautioned that, given the harsh processes of geological destruction and creation—"rivulets bringing down mud, and the waves wearing away the sea cliffs"—one should not expect to find abundant unbroken records of species' progressively developing ancestry (295).

As provocative as *Origin* would be at the time of its publication, Darwin omitted one immensely controversial topic: human origins. Although the implications for human origins were obvious from the book's arguments, Darwin didn't extend his argument explicitly until he published *Descent of Man* twelve years later in 1871, in which he argued that modern man descended from African hominids. By that time, Darwin had already suffered so much hostility for his evolutionary theories that any incremental criticism might not have fazed him much.

Although *Origin* was propounding an affirmative theory of origins, Darwin left no doubt that he was also debunking what he saw as its principal rival: creationism. The word *creation* appears about sixty times in *Origin*, always in a negative sense or as an argument or assumption to be refuted. Frequently, Darwin pointed out facts in the natural world that he found inconsistent with creation by an intelligent designer. For example, noting the immense varieties among species, he argued:

> Why, on the theory of Creation, should there be so much variety and so little real novelty? Why should all the parts and organs of many independent beings, each supposed to have been separately created for its proper place in nature, be so commonly linked together by graduated steps? Why should not Nature take a sudden leap from structure to structure? On the theory of natural selection, we can clearly understand why she should not; for natural selection acts only by taking advantage of slight successive variations; she can never take a great and sudden leap, but must advance by short and sure, though slow steps. (184)

Elsewhere he sought to turn the fact of rudimentary or vestigial organs from an embarrassment for evolutionary theory into an embarrassment for creationists:

> On the view of descent with modification, we may conclude that the existence of organs in rudimentary, imperfect, and useless condition, or quite aborted, far from presenting a strange difficulty, as they assuredly do on the old doctrine of creation, might even have been anticipated in accordance with the views here explained. (433)

Although Darwin studiously avoided couching his arguments in religious terms or attacking any particular religious doctrine, *Origins* left little doubt that he considered his theory to banish "the old doctrine of creation."

Origin made an instantaneous splash. An editorial published in the London *Times* immediately after the book's release raved over the book's thesis, a "hypothesis as vast as it is novel."[11] Many scientists flocked to support Darwin's theory, although others hotly contested it. Popular reaction was often hostile. Although *Origin* had not extended the evolutionary argument to man, as we have noted, the inference was not hard to draw and people quickly took umbrage at the suggestion that they had descended from apes. Cartoon portrayals of Darwin with a monkey's body became popular. Nonetheless, the book became an instant best-seller and Darwin's ideas rapidly spread throughout England, Europe, and the United States. In short order, Darwinism became the foundational theory underlying entire programs of research in biology, ecology, and many other fields of scientific and nonscientific inquiry and thought.

Except in the church, of course, where Darwinism was accorded the welcome of a vampire dropping in at a blood bank.

DARWINISM AND CHRISTIANITY: THREE LEVELS OF CONFLICT

As noted in the quotation at this chapter's beginning, in the waning pages of *Origin*, Darwin expressed the view that his arguments should not offend anyone's religious sensibilities. The very last sentence of *Origin* sought to leave open some space for an original Creator who had "breathed" life into a few original life forms and then stepped out of the way to let evolution run its course. But Darwin was well aware that he was challenging traditional Christian views and that the church would quickly react. It did.

The story of conflict between Darwinism and Christianity is so well-known that it is easy to lose track of the precise ways in which Darwinism conflicted with an orthodox Christian worldview. Given the breathtakingly broad implications of evolutionary theory, the points of potential conflict with Christian thinking are many. For simplicity, however, we can lump the conflicts into three broad categories.

First, Darwin's account of the origins of life through natural selection clashed with a literal interpretation of Scripture, most particularly the Genesis account of the special creation of the world in six days. Most Christians of Darwin's time believed that the days of the Genesis account were literal twenty-four-hour periods and that the earth was young—in the neighborhood of six thousand years old. Most of all, Christians believed that the book of Genesis taught that God had directly created the separate species of the world through his supernatural powers. A naturalistic account of the origin of species through random, unguided processes spread over millions of years seemed to contradict their interpretation of the Genesis account.

If Darwin's theories did contradict the Bible, then this would mount a serious challenge to orthodox Christian doctrine—which holds that the Bible is entirely true, inerrant, and comprehensively authoritative. It would not do to admit that biblical authors had erred in some scientific matter unimportant to the rest of Christian doctrine. Since Christians believe the Scriptures to be God's divinely inspired word, once any jot or tittle is shown to be erroneous, the entire structure of orthodox Christian belief collapses, especially for those in the Protestant tradition who venerate scriptural authority above all else. When it comes to the integrity of Scripture, it doesn't matter if the error concerns the fact of Jesus' resurrection or the middle name of one of David's mighty men. Any error, great or small, bursts the dike.

If Darwin's theories were right, then the only way to save the Genesis account—and by extension the entire system of belief built on biblical inerrancy and authority—was to reinterpret the Genesis account in nonliteral terms. Genesis might be giving a poetic rather than scientific account of life's origins. Backing away from literalism might seem an easy move. Literalism is easy to mock as an interpretive mode, since it so often produces absurd results. In the Scopes Monkey Trial, even William Jennings Bryan conceded that not every statement in the Bible should be taken literally. When Jesus said that his followers were "the salt of the earth," he obviously didn't mean that they were literally sodium chloride. He was speaking metaphorically, Bryan conceded.

But orthodox Christians felt that they could not concede more than a few inches of turf to metaphorical or aliteral biblical interpretations without risking the entire field. Nineteenth-century German higher criticism was already provoking controversy in the church by subjecting Scripture to rationalistic and secular interpretive methods that threatened to upend longstanding theological traditions. Make the first few chapters of Genesis mere metaphors, and the church would be off to the races on the rest of Scripture. What other stories, commandments, doctrines, or prophecies might be "mere metaphors" if the Genesis creation account were reduced to a metaphor or poetic account? All the miracles? The virgin birth? The resurrection of Jesus? The second coming? For orthodox Christians, Darwin's account of evolution through natural selection threatened to destabilize an entire system of authority, belief, and practice.

A second way in which *Origin of Species* rocked Christian thinking was in its implications for the origins, nature, and place of man in the world. Although, as already noted, Darwin stopped short in *Origin* of suggesting an evolutionary origin for man, the implication was obvious. Man, being just another mammal, would have descended from a predecessor organism through the random process of natural selection. The provocation of this Darwinian implication went far beyond its clash with a literal interpretation of the Genesis account of God's creation of Adam from the dust of the earth and of Eve from Adam's rib. The dethronement of man from his place as a special creation in the image of God created both theological and moral problems of the profoundest nature.

Holding man to be a spontaneous product of nature presented a grave theological problem for the entire scriptural narrative of creation, fall, and redemption. The historicity of Adam, the progenitor of the human race, and his relationship to Jesus, "the second Adam," had long been pillars of Christian theology. For example, the fifth chapter of Paul's Epistle to the Romans creates a parallel between Adam and Jesus as historical individuals who played critical roles in the arc of human history: Just as sin entered the world through the wrongful choice of a one man, Adam, so salvation came through the righteous life and death of another man, Jesus. Evolutionary theory necessarily dispensed with a historical Adam. There might be a Mitochondrial Eve and Y-chromosomal Adam—the most recent matrilineal and patrilineal ancestors of all human beings identified through contemporary DNA evidence—but no possibility of a single created individual who, taking forbidden fruit from his wife, brought sin upon the human race. And if there were no literal, historical Adam who brought sin, then why would there need to be redemption through a single, historical person like Jesus? Evolutionary theory thus threatened the narrative stability of conventional Christian story of redemptive history, including the central place of Jesus Christ himself.

In addition, many Christians believed that the demotion of man from divine image-bearer to "ape" created a moral crisis. In its crassest version, this concern found expression in the anti-Darwinist maxim that if you teach children that they are descended from monkeys, then they will begin to behave like monkeys. More generally, Christians fretted that Darwin's brutal account of origins based on the survival of the fittest encouraged an ethic of ruthless, amoral selfishness. If man was just another product of nature—and nature was, as Alfred Lord Tennyson poetically described it, "red in tooth and claw"—then what hope was there for altruism, civility, morality, and decency?

Although *Origin* was a work on natural science, not a moral argument, as decades passed and Darwinism gained wide acceptance, critics pinned more and more social, political, and moral theories—some of which were decidedly contrary to Christian doctrine—on Darwin's ideas. In Darwin's defense, it was impossible that all of these views were direct results of Darwinist ideas, since some of them were diametrically opposed to others. For example, Darwinism has sometimes been credited with inspiring both Marxism and free-market capitalism. Karl Marx (studied next in chapter 5) was a great admirer of Darwin and, in 1873, sent him an inscribed copy of *Das Kapital*.[12] But the theory of evolution through natural selection was equally important in the "social Darwinist" thought of Herbert Spencer, the English philosopher who, more than any other, justified the laissez faire economic and social policies of Victorian England. It was Spencer, not Darwin, who coined the phrase "survival of the fittest" after reading *Origin of Species*. That both communism and capitalism lie at the feet of Darwinism seems implausible.

Nonetheless, Christian opponents of Darwinism were surely correct to worry about uses some people would make of Darwin's scientific claims—whether or not *Origin* actually lent support to those uses. Many of Darwin's adherents, including his son Leonard, became involved in the now-discredited eugenics movement, which sought to better the human race through such brutal tactics as forced sterilization. At the extreme, Nazi Germany's racist ideology and justifications of racial genocide loudly echoed Darwinist themes of struggle for survival and racial improvement through ruthless supremacy. Darwinism might be only a scientific theory on its face, but Christian critics quickly saw how it could transmutate into deeply subversive ideological theories by eliminating the biblical view of man as a sacred moral agent reflecting the image of God.

A third broad category of Christian objection concerned evolutionary theory's implications for God. It was bad enough that Darwinism demoted man from a semi-divine being to a mere "ape," but the theory implied even worse as to God—that he was superfluous to the natural order and perhaps even a myth. Darwin's offering at the end of *Origin*—that maybe, just maybe, God had created the first simple organisms before turning over the enterprise of propagation and change to natural, incremental processes—left room for Deism at most. Theism—a role for an active God directly and continually engaged with his creation—was not in Darwin's cards. Gone was the God of redemptive history, a God who sent a great flood, confused language at Babel, parted the Red Sea, made the sun stand still, shut the lions' mouths, intervened in the fiery furnace, and, ultimately, sent his own Son to redeem a creation corrupted by sin. At best, Darwinism left God as the clockmaker who wound up his invention and then stepped away to let it run on its own. At worst, evolutionary theory seemed to suggest that clocks could come into being spontaneously, cutting out the clockmaker altogether.

Many Christians believed that Darwinism was indistinguishable from atheism. In the words of the Princeton theologian Charles Hodge in 1874, Darwinism "is atheism" and "the denial of God."[13] Although Darwin himself denied this, many of his successors eventually took up that claim with enthusiasm, arguing that Darwinism had indeed rendered God and religion obsolete. (More on this in a moment.) Whether or not Darwin's scientific theories actually required atheism, the church was not crazy to fear that Darwinism as an intellectual school would eventually veer in that direction.

THE CHURCH'S (GENERALLY) FEROCIOUS RESPONSE

Not all Christians reacted to Darwinism with horror. Some even embraced it with enthusiasm. Of particular importance were the pro-Darwinist arguments of the Harvard botanist Asa Gray, an orthodox Presbyterian, and one of the most important American natural scientists of the nineteenth century. Gray enthusiastically propounded Darwinism, seeing no conflict with Christianity and indeed an important role for God in guiding the course of evolution. Gray's theistic evolution theories provided cover for Christians to accept Darwinism as valid science, and some other Christian intellectuals stated their acceptance of the theory. But most leading Christians in England and the United States declined the cover, preferring a brawl.

The fierce backlash began almost immediately upon the publication of *Origin*. The stage was set in a famous encounter between Samuel Wilberforce, the Lord Bishop of Oxford, and British biologist Thomas Huxley, who became known as "Darwin's bulldog" for his tenacious defense of Darwin's theories. In 1860, hundreds of Oxford intellectuals crowded into the Oxford University Museum of Natural History for a meeting of the British Association for the Advancement of Science. Word had spread that Wilberforce (like Bryan a generation later, one of the leading orators of his day) would use the meeting to denounce Darwinism, with Huxley as his direct target in the audience. Sure enough, Wilberforce launched into a tirade against Darwinism, ostensibly on scientific grounds. According to popular reports (which have been disputed as to some details), Wilberforce then made the argument personal, calling out Huxley and demanding to know whether he was descended from a monkey on his mother's or his father's side.[14] Huxley hotly replied that he wouldn't be ashamed to have a monkey as an ancestor, but he would be ashamed to be connected with someone who used deceptive oratory to suppress scientific truth. The tenor for the next century and a half's skirmishing had been set.

Although Wilberforce's arguments were couched in scientific terms, many Christians quickly abandoned the idea of disputing Darwinism with scientific criticism, opting instead for theological arguments, vitriolic rhetoric, or both. Leading voices cast the debate as the battle of the age between God and Satan. This was particularly true in the United States, with the rise of Christian fundamentalism in the late nineteenth and early twentieth century. In sermons, books, pamphlets, and speeches, prominent Christian leaders torpedoed evolution in rhetoric that made Jesus' sharpest words—brood of vipers, whitewashed sepulchers—seem warm and fuzzy. The evangelist Billy Sunday, introduced earlier in this chapter, proclaimed that Darwin was burning in hell, that evolution was "chained to the Devil's throne," and that believers in evolution were "godless bastards and losers."[15] John Roach, pastor of Calvary Baptist Church in New York City, preached that "the great battle of the age is now on between Christianity and evolution." He argued that it would be "better to wipe out all of the schools" than to let any school teach children evolution.[16] The flamboyant Los Angeles evangelist Aimee Semple McPherson delivered sermons to vast in-person and radio audiences, denouncing evolution as "Satanic intelligence" and comparing Darwin to Hitler.[17] The evangelist William B. Riley decried Darwinism as "propaganda of infidelity, palmed off in the name science." Many Christian theologians and evangelists whose work remains revered in the American evangelical tradition today, men such as D. L. Moody and Charles Spurgeon, spoke out fiercely against evolutionary theory as a spiritual and moral seduction of Satan.

American Christians, however, were not content to battle Darwinism in the marketplace of ideas. Three states—Tennessee, Mississippi, and Arkansas—passed laws prohibiting the teaching of evolution in public schools, and other states passed laws making it difficult to teach evolution (for example, by restricting discussion of evolution in science textbooks). As noted in the introduction, the Scopes Monkey Trial brought worldwide attention to these laws and the ostensible clash between science and the Bible that Darwinism represented. Although the trial invigorated anti-Darwinist Christians, over time it became a popular symbol of everything backwards about Christian fundamentalism. In 1968, the United States Supreme Court struck down the Arkansas law in *Epperson v. Arkansas*, holding that such statutes violated the provision of the Constitution's First Amendment prohibiting governments from establishing a religion. In 1987, the court visited the flipside of the issue—a Louisiana statute requiring that schools teach creationism—and held such laws also unconstitutional. After over a century of battling, Darwinism had finally won the battle for the public schools.

Christians were not easily deterred by these setbacks. Resistance to having children exposed to evolution was an important factor in the dramatic rise of homeschooling—from about ten thousand children in the 1970s to over two million today—and the growth in evangelical Christian private schools (even as enrollment in Catholic parochial schools declined). Although the teaching of evolution was only one factor in these shifts, Darwin's theories clearly contributed to the ongoing separation of many conservative Christians from popular culture.

As their defeats in the courts of law and public opinion mounted, some anti-evolutionary Christians felt the need to mount a quasi-secular intellectual counterinsurgency rather than one based solely on the authority of Scripture. The Institute for Creation Research, founded in 1970 and associated with popular Christian author Tim

LaHaye, launched a campaign to muster scientific evidence supporting the Genesis creation account, or at least a fairly literal interpretation of it. While the center has attracted support from some well-credentialed scientists, mainstream scientists have often derided the institute's work as pseudo-science, or religion masquerading as science.

Over time, Christian anti-Darwinists began to shift their focus from defending the Genesis account in scientific terms to attacking the Darwinist account in scientific terms. Instead of arguing for creationism as revealed in Scripture, some Christians began to argue that scientific inquiry reveals "intelligent design," evidence that the physical universe was designed by an intelligent engineer rather than generated through random chance. Intelligent design proponents seek to expose scientific gaps and inconsistencies in Darwin's theories, but without necessarily demanding a quasi-literal interpretation of Genesis as its replacement.

Phillip Johnson, a law professor at the liberal University of California Berkeley, oddly enough has been one of the leading Christian proponents of intelligent design. His 1991 book *Darwin on Trial* (which to date has sold over 250,000 copies) raises a number of questions about the sufficiency of evolutionary theory to explain the biological origins. Johnson does not question whether some degree of evolution—what we might call microevolution—occurs, but he does question whether Darwinian theory is sufficient to show that macroevolution—the change from one species to another—occurs through random chance. Johnson focuses on a number of issues that Darwin himself anticipated, such as the problem of "saltation," or sudden leaps from one species to another, and the continued meagerness of support for Darwin's theories in the fossil record.

Johnson's book reenergized Darwin skeptics, hungry for a well-credentialed secular academic (albeit a nonscientist) to take down Darwin on his own rationalistic terms. Equally, Johnson's book outraged Darwinists in the scientific community who view ostensibly rationalist skepticism about Darwinism as a covert play for anti-rationalist, anti-scientific religious dogma. The scientific establishment's bombastic attack on Johnson has rivaled in tone the early Christian criticisms of Darwin. For example, Stephen Jay Gould's review of *Darwin on Trial* asserts that it is "abysmally written" and a "mixture of ignorance and inappropriateness," and that it "hardly deserves to be called a book at all." This was not very charitable, but then again neither was the Christian attack on Darwin.

FRONTIERS OF DARWINISM AND CHRISTIAN THOUGHT

Darwinism has flourished with the exponential power of an advantaged genetic trait. The theory is now so firmly established in biological science that the scientific establishment deems it virtually unquestionable. This is not to say that every aspect of *Origin* remains untouchable, or that scientists agree on every aspect of evolutionary theory. Sharp clashes within the scientific community persist; for example, on such matters as whether evolution occurs more at the genetic level (as argued by the Oxford biologist Richard Dawkins) or at the organism level (as argued by the Harvard paleontologist Stephen Jay Gould). Science has also refined and updated Darwin's accounts of the evolutionary process in important ways. A crucial ingredient missing from Darwin's account was the means by which parents transmit idiosyncratic traits to their offspring. Unaware of the gene, Darwin confessed ignorance on how differences arose within a species, and therefore he could not account for the mechanisms of transmission. Gregor Mendel, a contemporary of Darwin's and an Augustinian friar and abbot in what is now the Czech Republic, developed theories that would lead to the modern science of genetics and supply Darwin's missing pieces. The synthesis between Darwin's theory of natural selection and Mendelian rules of inheritance is called the modern synthesis, and it underlies much—some would say all—of modern biological science.

If the scientific establishment now holds that the case for Darwinism is settled, what about the church? Although generalizations can be perilous, at the level of rhetoric and willingness to listen, the overall trend of the past few decades has been a softening by the church and a hardening by secular skeptics. With important exceptions, one comes away today with the impression that the church is willing to listen to science but that science isn't so willing to listen to the church.

The Catholic Church has largely made its peace with Darwin. In 1950, in the encyclical *Humani generis*, Pope Pius XII wrote that there is no essential conflict between Christianity and Darwinism, so long as Christians adhere to the church's teaching that God creates individual human souls. Since most secular scientists don't particularly believe in ethereal souls—or have nothing scientific to say about them if they do—this formulation manages to allocate jurisdiction between science and the church in a way that minimized the potential for future showdowns.

In the United States, mainline Protestant churches have long made their own peace with evolution, leaving the battle to fundamentalists and evangelicals. Evangelicals have not abandoned the fight, although their tone and vehemence has somewhat softened. Pew Forum research data suggests that about two-thirds of white evangelical Protestants and half of African-American Protestants still reject the theory of evolution, believing that man has existed in his present state since the beginning of time. Conversely, about a third of white evangelicals and half of African-American Protestants do believe that man descended from other life forms—a finding that itself would have rocked the church just a few decades ago.

Two men who served, respectively, as the intellectual and pastoral high priests of American evangelicalism in the postwar era came to peace with the core *scientific* claims of Darwinism. In various writings, C. S. Lewis, the British author of *Mere Christianity* and the beloved Narnia books, made it clear that he had no objection to evolution—including the descent of man from other animals—as a scientific theory, saving his objections for various moral claims arising from Darwinism. Similarly, the American evangelist Billy Graham deliberately avoided provoking controversies over evolutionary theory. In his 1997 book *Personal Thoughts of a Public Man*, Graham argued that the Bible was not a scientific book so there was no conflict between the Bible and science, that the appearance of conflicts mostly had to do with misinterpretations of Scripture, and that whether God created man through "an evolutionary process" or not "makes no difference as to what man is and man's relationship to God."[18] Many other Christian leaders, although certainly not all, called for Christians to back away from antagonism against the science of evolution and to focus instead on the disturbing moral, theological, and social claims arising from various interpretations of evolution.

Even while the church was largely shifting away from all-out war with Darwinism, secular skeptics were taking Darwinism where Darwin himself denied it should go: into not just an alternative to a literal account of Genesis but to a refutation of the existence of God altogether. Richard Dawkins, an evolutionary biologist and Oxford professor, and Daniel Dennett, a Tufts University philosopher, have played leading roles in validating Charles Hodge's earlier assertion that Darwinism means atheism—although, unfortunately, they mean it as a good thing! In his 1995 book *Darwin's Dangerous Idea*, Dennett asserts that Darwinism is not only a scientific idea about the origins of life but also a pervasive philosophical idea that grounds every other philosophical idea and provides the only *meaning* of life. Darwinism, he argues, necessarily requires abandoning any belief in a personal God:

> The kindly God who lovingly fashioned each and every one of us (all creatures great and small) and sprinkled the sky with shining stars for our delight—*that* God is, like Santa Claus, a myth of childhood, not anything a sane, undeluded adult could literally believe in.[19]

Similarly, Dawkins argues in his 2006 best-seller *The God Delusion*, that the existence or nonexistence of God is a scientific fact about the universe, that evolution by natural selection eliminates any reason to believe that the universe is designed and, hence, that Darwinism eliminates any reason to believe in God.

As the twenty-first century dawned, it became increasingly apparent that the ultimate project of many *Darwinists*, if not *Darwin* himself, was to take down orthodox Christianity altogether. A telling example arose in 2014 in a debate between Ken Ham, president of the creationist organization Answers in Genesis, and Bill Nye, a science educator and TV personality ("Bill Nye the Science Guy") and leading critic of creationism. Nye spent most of the debate offering traditional scientific arguments against creationism and in favor of evolution in a measured, scholarly tone. But at one point he veered off the script of science and laid into the Christian doctrine that those who do not accept Jesus as Savior are damned to hell. If Nye's goal was to persuade viewers that they should allow their understanding of the natural world to be guided by "objective" scientific principles and leave issues faith or belief to the realm of religion or morals (essentially the *Humani generis* compromise), this was a colossal strategic error. The slip-up suggested that Nye's problem wasn't just with creationism for scientific reasons, but with Christianity for moral reasons completely detached from science. It's hard for scientists to protest when the clergy meddle in scientific matters when scientists themselves are meddling in religious matters. Then, again, if Dawkins and Dennett are correct that science and religion are *not* detached disciplines but rather mutually exclusive ways of understanding . . . everything . . . then Nye's attack on the doctrine of damnation was not out of bounds. It wasn't out of bounds, because there are no bounds.

To be sure, the case that accepting Darwinism as a scientific theory of origins requires accepting Darwinism as a philosophy and rejecting theism does not yet have broad support among important thinkers, whether Christian or secular. In 2011, Calvin College professor and renowned philosopher Alvin Plantinga published *Where the Conflict Really Lies: Science, Religion, and Naturalism,* which systematically dismantles any such arguments and shows, to the contrary, that modern scientific theories fit comfortably with a theistic worldview. Still, it is hard to escape the conclusion that the way the church attacked Darwinism historically facilitated the rise of claims such as Dawkins's and Dennett's.

In *The Scandal of the Evangelical Mind,* church historian Mark Noll's highly influential critique of evangelical anti-intellectualism, Noll rightly observes that Christians' scathing antagonism toward Darwin's scientific claims deeply damaged Christians' ability to be heard on the "philosophical pretensions of grand-scale Darwinistic theories."[20] It's awkward, at best, for Christians to argue that evolution through natural selection as a generally accepted scientific theory doesn't destroy the Bible's credibility or require atheism when, for decades, they vehemently argued just the opposite. Recall the anti-Darwinist maxim that said if you tell children they are descended from monkeys, then they will start to act like monkeys. Is it possible that telling Darwinists that they are descended from an atheist has made them start to act like atheists? Certainly, some skeptics would have come around to atheistic extensions of Darwinism even if the church's response had been more measured. But there can be little doubt that the church's response to *Origin of Species* made being heard on scientific, philosophical, and other intellectual matters much more challenging than it needed to be.

CHAPTER 5

Karl Marx's *Communist Manifesto*: The Red Bull of the Masses

*"Religion is the sigh of the oppressed creature, the
heart of a heartless world, and the soul of soulless
conditions. It is the opium of the masses."*

Karl Marx
*A Contribution to the Critique of Hegel's Philosophy of
Right* (written in 1843, published posthumously)

On April 12, 1961, at the height of the Cold War, the Russian astronaut Yuri Gagarin flew into outer space for 108 minutes and then returned safely to earth. He was the first man in space. The Soviet leadership exulted in this triumph of Communist ideology and made Gagarin the poster boy of Soviet propaganda. To the Soviets, it wasn't simply a triumph of science and engineering. It was also a triumph of Marxist ideology. For, as Soviet Premier Nikita Khrushchev boasted and a Kremlin propaganda poster proclaimed, Gagarin reported that out in space he looked around and didn't see God.

As with so many ideological vignettes, this one was fabricated. Years later, after Gagarin's death and the end of the Cold War, it came out that Gagarin was actually a baptized member of Russian Orthodox Church, a quiet believer in God, and had never uttered those words. But never mind the facts. The story was too poignant to ignore, and it spawned its own coterie of stories and extensions.

In response to the (fabricated) Gagarin quote, a long sequence of American astronauts mounted an overwhelming counteroffensive. Frank Borman, commander of the first space crew to travel beyond the earth's orbit, radioed back the first verse of Genesis: "In the beginning, God created the heavens and the earth." Shortly before Neil Armstrong and Buzz Aldrin stepped onto the moon in their "giant leap for mankind," Aldrin slipped out a few items in the lunar module—a Bible, a silver chalice, and bread and wine—and took the first lunar Communion. James Irwin, who walked on the moon in 1971, later became a Christian minister and insisted that on the moon, "I felt the power of God as I'd never felt it before."[1]

These dueling interpretations of the religious meaning of space travel were just one vignette in the greatest ideological conflict that humanity has ever witnessed—that between Soviet Marxist Communism and Western capitalist democracy. There were many facets to this great contest—politics, social organization, economics, technology, military might, and, of course, religion. In a crude but viscerally real sense, Marxism stood for atheism and Western democracy for the Judeo-Christian tradition: thus the calculated propaganda war over the admittedly silly question of whether God could be seen in space.

How did Marxism become so associated with atheism? That linkage is not inevitable. As we shall see, there have been philosophical and practical political movements to create a Christian version of Marxism, most notably the South American liberation theology movement of the 1950s and '60s. Marxism did not necessarily have to equate to atheism, and yet in its dominant forms it did. How did this come about?

The story begins with a nineteenth-century Jewish boy, baptized for business reasons as a Christian in Prussia, who went on to become the world's most famous anti-Christian revolutionary. Karl Marx's three-volume *Das Kapital* laid out a "scientific" critique of capitalism and the dense, economic theory of what would become known as "Marxism." But it was *The Communist Manifesto*, a short pamphlet that Marx co-wrote with his long-time collaborator and financial backer, Friedrich Engels, that stoked the fires of revolution. The *Manifesto* famously ended with a call for the workers of the world to unite. This inflammatory call to action was necessary, Marx argued, because the proletariat had become lulled into bondage by a drug that had dulled their senses and made them unable to realize the true sources of their misery. That opiate was religion. For the revolution to take root, religion must be destroyed.

Atheistic Communism,—and its most sinister instantiations in Bolshevism, Stalinism, and Maoism—not only rocked the church intellectually. For millions of Christians living behind the Iron Curtain or in other Communist regimes, Marxism and its descendants meant severe persecution or death. And although political Marxism faded after the fall of the Berlin Wall in 1989, it is far from moribund. Now, as much as ever, Marxism challenges the church.

THE MAKING OF A REVOLUTIONARY

Karl Marx was born in Prussia in 1818, only a few decades after Voltaire, whom we met in chapter 3, quit the Prussian court of Frederick the Great in disgrace. Karl's father, Heinrich Marx, a lawyer, was the son of a prominent rabbi and Talmudic scholar, and his mother was also the daughter of a rabbi. Nonetheless, when a Prussian edict in 1816 banned Jews from advancement in the legal profession, Heinrich had the whole family baptized as Christians. Heinrich has been described as "a real eighteenth century Frenchman, who knew his Voltaire and Rousseau inside and out."[2] In time, Karl would as well.

Karl Marx never embraced his Jewish heritage and, for a time, seemed to be a zealous Christian. An essay Marx wrote at the age of seventeen as he graduated from a formerly Jesuit high school speaks of the happiness "which only one bound unconditionally and child-like to Christ, and through him to God, can know."[3] Some of his early writings would come across as positively anti-Semitic. Marx argued that Judaism had seduced Christianity into an avaricious love of money and finance, and that this corruption could be undone only by revolutionary social and economic upheaval: "In emancipating itself from hucksterism and money, and thus from real and practical Judaism, our age would emancipate itself."[4]

Marx received his university education in law and philosophy in Bonn and Berlin, where he joined drinking clubs and poetic societies and engaged in dueling. Along the way, he also managed to win the hand of Jenny von Westphalen, a baroness far above Marx's petty bourgeois station. Ironically, Marx's life work was largely financed by family relations to Philips Electronics and other major industrial ventures and by his collaborator, Friedrich Engels, who hailed from a wealthy industrial family with factory interests in Germany and England. Marx may have hated capitalism, but it made possible his life. As a young man, Marx borrowed recklessly and was frequently indebted to high-interest money lenders, which stoked his fury against the practice of usury. A long (and anti-Semitic) anti-usury passage in *Das Kapital* is largely culled from an anti-usury tract by Martin Luther.[5] The self-styled champion of the working man, Marx never held a regular job and lived off of family legacies and loans from benefactors.

While living in Berlin and finishing his academic studies, Marx became interested in the work of the German philosopher Friedrich Hegel, whose dialectic interpretation of history heavily influenced Marx's development of the theory of historical materialism. Hegel argued that history had to be understood as a pattern of contestation between a predominant thesis, challenged by an antithesis, which gives rise to a solution or synthesis. In *The Communist Manifesto* and *Das Kapital*, Marx appropriated this understanding of history to explain the rise of capitalism, its inevitable confrontation with Communism, and its eventual resolution into Communism.

Marx's study of Hegel led him to write a paragraph-by-paragraph critique of Hegel's *Elements of the Philosophy of Right*, which was published after Marx's death as a *Critique of Hegel's Philosophy of Right*. It is here that we find Marx's most comprehensive and poignant critique of religion. Religion, argued Marx, is an illusory creation of human society that simultaneously protests real suffering and furthers real suffering by disguising its economic and social causes. It is the "opium of the people" in the sense that it dulls people to the true sources of their unhappiness and prevents them from taking action to uproot these sources. Hence, "the abolition of religion as the *illusory* happiness of the people is the demand for their *real* happiness."[6]

In his critique of Hegel, Marx also introduced a "theory of alienation," which he borrowed in concept from the German philosopher Ludwig Feuerbach, and which would become important to his subsequent critique of capitalism. In a society stratified by class, Marx argued, workers become mechanistic units of production and therefore estranged or alienated from important aspects of their human essence.

While he was developing his political and economic ideas, Marx and Jenny lived as stateless drifters, moving from Berlin to Cologne, to Paris, to Brussels, back to Cologne, and eventually to London, where he would settle in older age. Increasingly, he fell in with political radicals, particularly socialists and Communists who challenged the existing European order through labor organization and potentially armed uprising. It was in Paris in 1844 that Marx met his eventual collaborator on the creation of the Communist League and his co-author of the *Communist Manifesto*, Engels, at the Café de la Régence.

In February 1848, on the cusp of a "Year of Revolution" in Europe, Marx and Engels published *The Communist Manifesto*—their call for worldwide revolt of the proletariat, which we shall examine in greater detail momentarily. The *Manifesto* was published by the Workers' Educational Association in London in German, with other translations soon to follow. Shortly thereafter, the first of the 1848 popular revolutions broke out in France against the government of King Louis-Philippe. Anti-monarchical, pro-labor, and pro-democracy revolutions quickly engulfed the rest of Europe, with widespread violence and tens of thousands of casualties resulting before the established governments restored order. The *Manifesto*, which had not yet reached most of the trouble spots at the time the violence erupted, played little direct role in the failed revolutions, but it finally tagged Marx as persona non grata to the major European governments. Marx was quickly expelled from Belgium and then in rapid succession from France and Prussia.

Like Voltaire before him and Freud after him, Marx found refuge in liberal, tolerant England, where he continued his scholarly work and revolutionary associations. Critics of Marx's philosophy often lampoon his ill manners and slovenly lifestyle. Early in his London years, Marx fell on particularly rough financial times (perhaps attributable to him refusing to work?), and his poor bourgeois wife had to put up with a disappointingly proletariat lifestyle. In 1850, the British ambassador to Berlin received the following colorful account of Marx's lifestyle in London from a Prussian spy snooping on German revolutionaries:

> [Marx] leads the life of a Bohemian intellectual. Washing, grooming and changing his linens are things he rarely does, and he is often drunk. Though he is frequently idle for days on end, he will work day and night with tireless endurance when he has much work to do. He has no fixed time for going to sleep or waking up. He often stays up all night and then lies down fully clothed on the sofa at midday, and sleeps until evening, untroubled by the whole world coming and going through his room.[7]

The report went on to describe Marx's apartment as scorched with tobacco and dilapidated: "Everything is dirty and covered with dust, so that to sit down becomes a hazardous business."[8]

While Marx's lifestyle may have been slovenly, it did afford him ample time to write. In addition to relying on Engels's largesse, Marx obtained some income as a foreign correspondent for the *New-York Daily Tribune* and several other newspapers. In 1867, Marx published the first volume of *Das Kapital*, the sole volume he would publish in his life. Engels would publish the second two volumes from Marx's notes after Marx's death, but it is the first volume that is famously associated with Marx's scathing critique of the capitalist mode of production, its oppression of the proletariat, and its inevitable demise into Communism. The uninitiated reader of *Das Kapital*, expecting a revolutionary screed akin to the *Communist Manifesto*, will be surprised to encounter a highly technical, and often scrupulously dense and boring, work of economics. It sketches (in sometimes mind-numbing detail) theories of wage labor, surplus value, declining rates of return on capital (profit), recession and depression, and the contradictory impulses of capitalism that give inexorable rise to proletariat revolution. Marx considered it a work of science rather than a normative prescription. His goal was to lay out a scientific basis for the inevitable collapse of capitalism and the rise of a socialist order.

The last decade of life brought Marx ill health and lower scholarly productivity, although he did still manage one of his more memorable turns of phrase—"from each according to his ability, to each according to his need"—in an 1875 missive to the Social Democratic Workers' Party of Germany. In 1883, Marx died at home in London following a prolonged illness. His grave remained in an obscure corner of Highgate Cemetery in London, until 1956 when a large marble block crowned by a cast-iron bust of Marx was erected to commemorate the man who had lit the world on fire. The epitaph on his tombstone presents one of Marx's saying for the ages:

> PHILOSOPHERS HAVE ONLY
> INTERPRETED THE WORLD IN
> VARIOUS WAYS—THE POINT
> HOWEVER IS TO CHANGE IT

Since his death, his admirers have frequently eulogized Marx as a man of great convictions, energy, and moral character. Yet, as with many people who achieve great fame, Marx had some serious personal blind spots. For all his concern about the exploitation of the working poor, Marx might have paid heed to Jesus' admonition to remove the plank out of one's own eye before pointing out the splinter in a brother's (Matthew 7:5). A peasant girl named Helen Demuth, or "Lenchen" as she was known, worked as a household servant to Marx from 1845 until her death in 1890, receiving room and board but never a penny of pay. Marx had an affair with Lenchen shortly after she joined his family, and then he refused to acknowledge the boy, Freddy, born from their illicit union. Lenchen had the boy fostered with another family, and he was allowed to visit the Marx residence, but he was forbidden to use the front door and could visit with his mother only in the kitchen.[9] As Paul Johnson notes, Lenchen and Freddy were perhaps the only real members of the proletariat Marx knew personally, and his treatment of them does not reflect well on the father of Communism.[10]

MARX'S CALL TO ARMS

The *Communist Manifesto* was commissioned by the Communist League at a congress held in London 1847 and assigned to Marx and Engels. Although the pamphlet appears under the name of both Marx and Engels, it was Marx's pen that scripted most of the document. Years after Marx's death, Engels acknowledged that while the *Manifesto* was "our joint production," "the fundamental proposition which forms its nucleus . . . belongs to Marx."[11]

Keying off the emerging crisis of 1848, the *Manifesto* begins with a short preamble describing the purpose and context of the document: "A specter is haunting Europe—the specter of Communism. All the powers of old Europe have entered into a holy alliance to exorcise this specter."[12] The choice of religious imagery here—Communism as a demonic force being exorcised by the Christian powers of Europe in holy alliance—is not coincidental. The Communists did not mind comparing themselves to demons as they meant to overthrow the entire existing order—church, state, and all.

Following its preamble, the *Manifesto* divides into four chapters. The first chapter, titled "Bourgeois and Proletarians," provides the organizing narrative of the Marxist view of history—dialectical materialism—and makes the *Manifesto*'s core claims. "The history of all hitherto existing society is the history of class struggles," it announces. Since the beginning of the world, the oppressed and oppressor have "stood in constant opposition to one another," fighting for control and constantly ending in either a revolutionary reconstitution of society or in mutual annihilation (9). Although this dialectic process had been going on forever, something had changed in the most recent iteration, something giving Marx assurance that the cycles of history were about to come to an end: The extreme differentiating effects of capitalism, in which the alienation of labor and capital had split society neatly into contending classes of capital-owning bourgeois and working proletarians, "has simplified the class antagonisms." "Society as a whole is more and more splitting up into two great hostile camps, into two great classes facing each other" (9). The bourgeois, themselves the winners in a dialectic action that overthrew feudalism merely a hundred years previously, had won the upper hand for the moment and now exploited the laboring class. But with the two classes squarely facing off, it was only a matter of time before the proletariat awoke from their slumber, saw the camps clearly, overthrew the bourgeois, and ended the vicious cycle once and for all.

One might quickly ask of Marx how he could be so certain that the proletariat would gain the upper hand and put an end to a history that Marx himself described as endlessly dialectical. Marx's answer is partly technical and partly simple head counting. The technical answer is this: Bourgeois capitalism depends on wage-labor exploitation. The wage-labor system rests on wage competition among workers, which impoverishes them so much that they begin to organize in labor unions to negotiate for better wages. This collective organization in unions breaks the workers' isolation, herds them into groups, and hence creates the organized vehicle by which the proletariat will overthrow the bourgeoisie. "What the bourgeoisie therefore produces above all, are its own grave diggers" (21). And why is the victory of the proletariat certain and its revolution equally certain not to be overtaken in a dialectic engagement with some new oppressor? In comes the head counting. In every prior historical movement, wrote Marx, minorities or the interests of minorities were the antagonists. But now "the proletarian movement is the self-conscious, independent movement of the immense majority, in the interest of the immense majority." The proletarian's victory and the demise of the bourgeois "are equally inevitable" (21).

The second chapter considers the relationship between the Communist Party and the proletarians of the world more generally. Marx and Engels give assurance that the Communist Party will advance the interests of all proletarians, regardless of national boundaries. Indeed, they assert that Communism will result in the abolition of nation states. They also respond to some criticisms of Communism.

One criticism is that Communism would destroy private property and freedom. Marx and Engels respond that the words *freedom* and *private property* have been perverted in the bourgeois capitalism order. "Freedom," in the sense of "free markets," only juxtaposes the capitalist system to the medieval system of restricted selling and buying. But the proletariat is far from "free" in the free market system (25). Similarly, the abolition of private property shouldn't cause any great concern, since nine-tenths of the people already own no private property. (A tremendous exaggeration, even for its time.)

Another criticism was that Communism would make people lazy. No, it's the bourgeois who are lazy, wrote Marx and Engels. Similarly, answering the reproach that Communism would lead to free love, the subjugation of women, and the abolition of the family, Marx and Engels turned the accusation back on the capitalists, accusing the bourgeoisie of moral looseness, the seduction of women, and instituting prostitution.

One final accusation—that Communism would destroy religion and with it conventional morality—met a different response, not of denial but of embrace. Traditional religion and the morality it expressed were simply the ideas of each age's ruling class. The ancient world was overcome by Christianity, and Christianity in turn by eighteenth-century Enlightenment rationalism. "The ideas of religious liberty and freedom of conscience, merely gave expression to the sway of free competition within the domain of knowledge." In other words, both ideas about religious freedom and religious ideas themselves were simply creations of the ruling class and, as such, were part and parcel of the "exploitation of one part of society by the other." Communism, "the most radical rupture with traditional property relations," also involved "the most radical rupture with traditional ideas"—including religion and morality (29). Chapter 2 ends with a series of demands, such as abolition of all private real estate, a heavy progressive or graduated income tax, abolition of all rights of inheritance, and universal free public education.

Chapter 3, of least ongoing interest, contrasts Communism with several other generally socialistic schools of thought that had arisen over time—i.e., Feudal Socialism, Petty Bourgeois Socialism, Critical-Utopian Socialism, and so on. One of these—Feudal Socialism—merits our attention because of its importance to Marx's views on Christianity. Marx and Engels invented the phrase "Feudal Socialism" to refer to the mid-nineteenth-century reform movements in France and England that arose in reaction to the rise of capitalism. These reformers, many of whom were drawn from the aristocracy, critiqued industrial capitalism as breaking down traditional social bonds and enabling anarchic, egotistical individualism. Marx and Engels argued that, although nominally anti-capitalist, Feudal Socialism entrenched the class relations of bourgeois and proletarian: "What [the Feudal Socialists] upbraid the bourgeoisie with is not so much that it creates a proletariat, as that it creates a *revolutionary* proletariat" (33; italics original). Much of Feudal Socialist movement had a Catholic Christian and Scholastic orientation, and Marx and Engels pounced venomously on a Clerical Socialism, which they saw as a reactionary handmaiden of Feudal Socialism:

> Nothing is easier than to give Christian asceticism a Socialist tinge.
> Has not Christianity declaimed against private property, against
> marriage, against the state? Has it not preached in the place of these
> charity and poverty, celibacy and mortification of the flesh, monastic
> life and Mother Church? Christian Socialism is but the holy water with
> which the priest consecrates the heart-burnings of the aristocrat. (33)

As we shall see, there have been various efforts over time to give Marxism a Christian face, to create a Christian version of Marx's revolutionary enterprise. Marx and Engels considered and categorically rejected such a possibility at the outset.

The *Manifesto*'s final chapter ends with some Realpolitik—an assessment of the political parties around the world with which the

Communists could work. Marx and Engels promise that the Communists will work with "every revolutionary movement against the existing social and political order of things"—reserving the right, however, to press for an ideologically pure revolution when the time is right (44). The *Manifesto* then culminates in its famous, ominous call to action: "Let the ruling classes tremble at a Communist revolution. The proletarians have nothing to lose but their chains. They have a world to win. Workers of the world, unite!" (44).

And many of them did.

CONFLICTS WITH CHRISTIANITY

Those of us who lived through the great struggle of the Cold War, the bitter oppression of the church behind the Iron Curtain and throughout the Communist world, and the eventual fall of the Berlin Wall and spiritual renewal of Eastern Europe may find it needless to consider how Marxism conflicted with Christianity. The Latin phrase *res ipsa loquitur* ("the thing speaks for itself") comes to mind. Yet it would be myopic to focus on only the visceral, historical, political, and material conflict between Marxism and Christianity without examining the underlying ideological and metaphysical conflicts. Since 1989, Marxism has largely dissolved as a political system, but it lives on—with vigor—as an ideology. Relatively few politicians or political systems claim the mantle of Marxism—in the United States or abroad—but Marxist patterns of thought continue to exert a powerful social influence. For the church, it's still game on.

Among the many possible ways to catalogue the ideological clashes between Marxism and Christianity, three issues stand out as most significant: (1) history, (2) human alienation, and (3) collectivism versus individualism.

First, history. Much in the same way that Darwinism displaced God as important to an account of living organisms, so Marx's dialectic materialism provided an explanation for history in which a living, active, sovereign God had become superfluous and, indeed, a hostile idea. According to Marx, (history should be understood as a succession of natural, material forces crashing into other forces and resolving inevitably in new forces.) The connection to Darwinism wasn't lost on Marx and Engels. In his 1888 introduction to the *Manifesto*, Engels explained that he and Marx were "destined to do for history what Darwin's theory has done for biology." Marx similarly viewed Darwin as providing "the natural-history basis for our view," although he sometimes worried whether Darwin's theories provided a sufficiently strong prediction of the inevitability of socialism.[13] (As we saw in the preceding chapter, Darwin's theories in fact were used to advocate laissez faire capitalism.) In short, Marx wanted to naturalize all of history in humanistic terms and strip out of historical understanding any reference to the transcendent, eternal, or divine. Religion, in Marx's view, was just another material force in the world, created by men, used by men, and eventually abolished by men.

The Christian, by contrast, believes in a sovereign God who is active in history, steering the course of events, rising up and throwing down kings and kingdoms, and directing all matters toward a final eschaton. The history of the world is not that of class struggle over the allocation of social resources, but of God's providential interaction with humanity from creation, to fall, to redemption. The physical or material world represents only a small, evanescent slice of reality. The facts of material history are but momentary actions in the wide sweep of eternity. Marx's dialectic materialism therefore directly contradicts the Christian understanding of history and its political, social, and moral consequences.

Second, Marxism and Christianity share a view of man as alienated from something important, but they differ dramatically as to what that is. Marx argued that the more man labored for wages, the more he became alienated from the products of his labor and hence from himself. Capitalism robs man of his soul by objectifying commodities—the fruits of labor—and hence objectifying the laborer himself. Religion does the same thing, Marx argued: "The more man places in God, the less he retains in himself."[14] In Marx's account, economic oppression, enabled by religion, was the root cause of man's alienation from himself, and Communist revolution was the force necessary to bring man back into a right moral relationship with himself. To overcome man's alienation, argued Marx, both private property and religion must be abolished.

The Christian concurs with the Marxist that man is deeply alienated, but finds him far less alienated from himself than from God and fellow human beings. In the biblical account, the great story of history is the fall of humanity, alienation from God, and redemption. The pathologies we observe in the world—war, murder, and injustice—are not products of man's separation from himself but his separation from his Creator, and hence his alienation from both God and other human beings. The Christian shares the Marxist's desire for man to be made whole, but by clinging to God and loving his fellow human rather than by rediscovering fellowship with his labor. In Christian theology, restoration comes not from reuniting oneself but from denying oneself, putting to death one's own flesh, loving the other as oneself. After all, Ephesians 5:29 reminds us that no one ever hated his own flesh, but he nourishes and cherishes it. The problem is not alienation from self but self-centeredness, and the solution is not self-realization but self-abdication.

Finally, Marxism clashed with Christianity on the question of collectivism versus individualism. Following Engels, Marx wanted to tell a scientific story in which a necessary progression of historical events would inevitably occur because of the deterministic actions and counteractions of groups. Human agency was therefore always collective and individual actions and identities unimportant. Indeed, Marx argued that individuals were subsumed into their class:

> The class in its turn achieves an independent existence over against the individuals, so that the latter find their conditions of existence predestined, and hence have their position in life and their personal development assigned to them by their class, become subsumed under it.[15]

Capitalists, no less than proletarians, simply play a part assigned to them by their class and therefore should not be considered as individuals with separately significant ideas, values, and experiences. Although Marx imagined that the abolition of class following the proletarian revolution might create the possibility of individuality, Marxism's historical and political focus negated any present importance to individuals, personal responsibility, or the moral worth of a single person. The collective (the group) was everything, whether as the force to be opposed (the bourgeoisie) or the force to be liberated (the proletariat).

Christianity, by contrast, holds the individual person to be the sacred repository of God's own image, a special creation knit in his mother's womb and ordained by his Creator to a unique path. Both sin and salvation entered the world through the actions of "one man" (Rom. 5:12). Jesus called individual disciples and followers to himself, exhorting them to leave their family groups to walk with him (Luke 14:26). Salvation is an individual enterprise—a person must be born again through individual repentance and faith in the Savior (John 3). Individual accountability and responsibility flow from individual moral worth: each person should carry his own load (Gal. 6:5), and whoever doesn't work doesn't eat (2 Thess. 3:10). The individual person cannot be subsumed into his class to play a social, moral, and political role assigned by that class, since Christ's work abolishes material distinctions among humanity and makes all believers one (Gal. 3:28).

Contrasting the biblical affinity for the individual with the Marxist affinity for the group raises the question of whether the contemporary Western Church has gone too far in the direction of economic, spiritual, and moral individualism. As pastor and theologian John Piper has observed, it is common to hear "warnings against Western individualism, and invitations to return to *biblical* corporatism."[16] After all, God dealt with Israel primarily as a nation and ordained the church to be "one body" (1 Cor. 12:12). The early church appears to have practiced a form of socialism in which all goods were held in common (Acts 2:44). (It is easy to get carried away with the latter statement—members of the church certainly shared many of their assets, but they also continued to own individual property that the church considered legally and morally their own. See the story of Ananias and Sapphira in Acts 5:1–10.)

In *Mere Christianity*, C. S. Lewis proposes a uniquely Christian approach to avoiding the twin errors of totalitarianism (or collectivism of the kind asserted by Marx) and radical individualism.

> The idea that the whole human race is, in a sense, one thing—one huge organism, like a tree—must not be confused with the idea that individual differences do not matter or that real people, Tom and Nobby and Kate, are somehow less important than collective things like classes, races, and so forth. Christianity thinks of human individu-

als not as mere members of a group or items in a list, but as organs in a body—different from one another and each contributing what no other could. On the other hand, when you are tempted not to bother about someone else's troubles because they are 'no business of yours,' remember that though he is different from you he is part of the same organism as you. If you forget that he belongs to the same organism as yourself you will become an Individualist. If you forget that he is a different organ from you, if you want to suppress differences and make people all alike, you will become a Totalitarian. But a Christian must not be either a Totalitarian or an Individualist.[17]

This is not the place to resolve the broader question of whether the contemporary church has gone overboard in the direction of individualism. At a minimum, Christianity's high regard for the moral and spiritual worth of the individual man and woman stands in sharp contrast to the hyper-collectivist—Lewis would say Totalitarian— impulses of Marxism and *The Communist Manifesto*. The subsequent history of Marxism in the twentieth century, in which millions of individuals (including many Christians) were slaughtered by Marxist dictators (such as Lenin and Stalin in the Soviet Union) for the supposed advancement of the proletarian revolution, showcases the dangers of justifying wrong to an individual in the name of the good of the group.

THE CHURCH'S BITTERLY DIVIDED RESPONSE

The church's response to the *Communist Manifesto* and the Marxist revolution it unleashed on the world varied considerably by time, place, and context. Overall, the church's response was hostile (often vehemently so), but the opposite effect, efforts to create a Christian version of Marxism, also took hold on occasion. In between these poles, some Christians accepted certain tenets of Marx's economic theories and calls for reform, while rejecting the atheistic, humanistic, and most radical philosophical and political aspects of his theories.

The Catholic Church condemned *The Communist Manifesto* almost immediately. In an 1849 encyclical, Pope Pius IX denounced Marxism as full of "wicked theories" and "pernicious fictions."[18] But

Pius's response arguably struck a wrong note in a politically fraught moment. Rather than acknowledging that Marx had tapped into legitimate grievances of the working poor, Pius told the poor to grin and bear it:

> Let Our poor recall the teaching of Christ Himself that they should not be sad at their condition, since their very poverty makes lighter their journey to salvation, provided that they bear their need with patience and are poor not only possessions, but in spirit too.[19]

At a time when the poor of Europe were suffering true destitution and hopelessness, the encyclical came across as tone deaf.

Over the next several decades, the Catholic Church's official position on Marxism softened somewhat. A 1864 book by Wilhelm von Ketteler, the archbishop of Mainz, titled *The Labor Question and Christianity*, argued that Marxism went too far by advocating transfer of the means of production from the private sector to the state, but that liberal capitalism resulted in social and economic injustices that should be redressed through workers' associations and governmental interventions on behalf of workers. Ketteler's arguments became official Catholic dogma when incorporated into an 1891 encyclical, *Rerum Novarum*, by Pope Leo XIII. The new encyclical reaffirmed the importance of property rights as against Marxism, but it also recognized that "the hard-heartedness of employers and the greed of unchecked competition" had reduced "the teeming masses of the laboring poor to a yoke little better than slavery itself," which needed correction by the regulatory powers of the state.[20] Marx had not persuaded the Catholic Church, but the ideological and political pressures of his *Manifesto* had forced the church to come to grips with the excesses of capitalism.

Lacking a centralized authority comparable to that of the Catholic Church, European Protestants were more divided in their reaction to Marxism. The German Lutheran Pastor Johann Hinrich Wichern, who led an "Inner Mission" to the poor, argued that the working poor were degraded by a lack of piety and morality rather than economic oppression. In 1871, he sounded the alarm against the International Workingmen's Association, "an atheist and communist foundation, . . . an association of war and hatred [with the goal of] the annihila-

tion of capital and its owners. . . . Its rules of behavior are the nega-
tion of all principles on which civilization rests."[21] By contrast, other
European Protestants claimed sympathy with much of Marx's economic theories and calls for dramatic social change. Writing in 1912,
the prominent Anglican theologian William Temple (who would go
on to become the archbishop of Canterbury) argued vociferously
against the evils of laissez-faire capitalism, demanded that Christians
assent to collectivism, asserted that Marxism "is the only theory which
I personally regard as seriously formidable," and endorsed Marx's
historical materialism, at least as to economics.[22]

In the United States, the church's reaction to Marxism can be
viewed in two waves: first, an early twentieth-century fundamentalist
reaction to the *philosophy* of Marxism, and second, a broader Cold
War era reaction to the *politics* of Marxism.

The church's reaction to Marxism took some time to kindle,
largely due to the fact that the fundamentalist movement of the late
nineteenth and early twentieth centuries was committed to a premil-
lennial theology that, initially at least, called for disengagement with
politics.[23] Independently of Marxism, the mainstream Social Gospel
movement of the early twentieth century took seriously the church's
obligation to work toward poverty alleviation. However, a deep an-
tipathy to Marxism as a philosophical matter arose in the wake of the
Bolshevik Revolution of 1917 in Russia and World War I, largely in
conjunction with the backlash against Darwinism. The fundamentalist movement explicitly linked Darwinism and Marxism, suggesting
that the two ideas were part and parcel of a single anti-Christian conspiracy. A 1923 article in *Moody Monthly* announced that "evolution
is Bolshevism in the long run. . . . It eliminates the idea of a personal
God, and with that goes authority in government, all law and order."[24]
Another fundamentalist publication sarcastically suggested a presidential campaign of the liberal pastor Harry Emerson Fosdick on
the Socialist ticket with Clarence Darrow (whom we met defending
evolution in chapter 4) as his running mate.[25] Some strands of the
anti-Marxist reaction descended into conspiracy theories, lumping
together a series of global villains including Jews, Catholics, and Socialists dedicated to the destruction of the Christian order.[26]

There is much irony in the fundamentalist linkage of Jews and
Catholics with Marxism. As we saw, although ethnically Jewish, Marx

wanted nothing to do with the religion of his birth, personally stoking up anti-Semitism by denouncing the monetary culture of the Jews as the corrupting force of Christian capitalism. Further, when American opposition to Marxism entered its second and more ferocious wave in the wake of World War II, it was in the hands of Senator Joseph McCarthy, an Irish Catholic.[27] During the "Red Scare" period of the late 1940s and early 1950s, McCarthy successfully mobilized conservative American Christendom against the specter of Communism that was creeping into American institutions. McCarthyism drew staunch support from the conservative wings of both Protestantism and Catholicism, highlighting a trend in the second half of the twentieth century in which, on social and political matters, the Catholic/ Protestant divide would be replaced by a right/left divide. Although McCarthyism was discredited, and is now widely considered a period of hysterical excess, the association of conservative Protestants and Catholics in opposition to Marxism marked a historically significant shift in American politics with long-lasting implications. For example, in recent decades, evangelical Protestants and conservative Catholics have worked seamlessly together in the pro-life movement and on such political fronts as judicial nominations, a development that traces some precedence to a common mid-twentieth century anti-Marxist commitment.

As we saw, although in the *Communist Manifesto* Marx warned Christians not to bother trying to appropriate his theories and create a Christian variety of Marxism, some Christians disregarded his admonition. Prominent theologians such as Karl Barth, Paul Tillich, and Reinhold Niebuhr attempted to construct socialist theologies largely patterned on Marx's writings. In 1915, early in his career, Barth asserted that "a real Christian must become a socialist [and] a real socialist must become a Christian"[28] and that "anti-Communism [is] as a matter of principle an even greater evil than Communism itself."[29] During the 1930s, Niebuhr even styled himself a "Christian Marxist."[30] (He later repudiated Marxism.)

Some Christians went so far as to put Marx's ideas into revolutionary political action under the banner of the cross. During the 1950s and '60s, a generation of Christian "liberation theologians," mostly based in pervasively Catholic Latin America, urged socialistic revolution in the name of Christ. A Communist defector, the former head of Romania's secret police, has asserted that the KGB created liberation theology in order to spread revolution to South America.[31] Whether or not that claim is overstated or even true, liberation theology contributed significantly to the Marxist revolutions or rebellions in places such as Nicaragua, Honduras, and El Salvador. For example, the Sandinista ideology of Nicaragua's Marxist revolution was laced with Christian theology and supported by many Nicaraguan Catholics.[32] Although official church doctrine dismissed liberation theology, it is only somewhat of an exaggeration to say that the Cold War proxy battles in Latin America in the 1970s and '80s pitted conservative, capitalist Christianity against radical Marxist Christianity.

How, then, should we judge the church's reaction to Marxism? At times callous, at times deeply prejudiced, at times hysterical, and at times naively accepting, the church failed to reply to Marx with a unified voice. It should have acknowledged the social evils he identified, expressed genuine concern for the poor, and at the same time rejected his materialism, radicalism, and atheism. It should have proposed genuine, Bible-based solutions to the real economic and political problems that fueled the twentieth century's revolutions. Perhaps more than any other thinker in history, Marx's theories divided the church into radically opposed factions that often elevated politics over theology. The curmudgeonly Marx would surely be frustrated to discover that the church he meant to destroy he had only succeeded in dividing.

MARXISM TODAY (NO, IT'S NOT OVER)

A century and a half after Marx and Engels published their *Communist Manifesto*, we no longer need to speculate about Marx's predictions and theories. Although contemporary Marxists often argue that Marxism hasn't been shown to be a failure because it hasn't ever been tried, that claim is hard to swallow in light of the decades-long experience with self-proclaimed Marxist states like the Soviet Union, China, and Cuba. When East Germans fed up with the Communist system began to rip down the Berlin Wall down in 1989, it was clear that Marxism as a political system had taken a fatal public relations blow. Vestiges of political Marxism survive in isolated states like Cuba and North Korea or in the official ideology of states like China that functionally have taken major steps away from Communism (if not in the direction of political freedom). But the collapse of the Soviet Union and fall of the Iron Curtain left little doubt that Marx and Engel's revolutionary spirit of 1848 had been quenched.

There are many complex and controversial explanations for how this all came about, and we cannot do them justice here. Two brief observations will have to suffice.

First, the political practice of Marxism never matched the radically egalitarian rhetoric of Marxism. The proletariat quickly learned that class privilege did not cease with Communism, and that some of their politically favored comrades enjoyed special stores and health-care facilities, foreign travel, automobiles, and luxurious country da-chas of which the ordinary proletarian could only dream. The reality of applied Marxism was summed up by George Orwell's poignant ob-servation in *Animal Farm* that "all animals are equal, but some animals are more equal than others," and the quip, attributed to John Ken-neth Galbraith, that under capitalism man exploits man and under Communism it's just the opposite. Further, to the extent that Marx-ism achieved any measure of equality, it did so by driving standards of living *down* rather than up. Some people might consent to purchas-ing economic equality at the price of reduced average well-being, but few would consent to purchase it at the price of common destitution. That the East built the Iron Curtain to keep its own people in rather than Westerners out rapidly became incontrovertible.

Second (hopefully without gloating), we can observe that Marx's vehemence toward Christianity was repaid by a special place for the church in the downfall of Communism. After Marx, Soviet Com-munism took an ever more aggressive anti-Christian turn. Vladimir Lenin would take Marx's disdain of religion to its zenith, asserting that "every religious idea, every idea of god, even every flirtation with the idea of god is unutterable vileness."[33] If he meant that Christianity represented an irrepressible threat to Communism, he was right. The Christian writer Aleksandr Solzhenitsyn broke the moral image of the Soviet Union in works such as *The Gulag Archipelago,* asserting that "men have forgotten God; that's why all this has happened." Behind the Iron Curtain, the church grew stronger through oppression. And, it was the elevation of a Pole—John Paul II—as pope that helped to legitimate Lech Wałęsa's fledgling Solidarity movement, which in turn provided one of the first fractures in the Stalinist hegemony of the Soviet Union and its vassal states.

Yet if Marxism has suffered a dire political reversal since 1989, it still carries on a powerful influence in various walks of life. "Even today," wrote Louis Menand in *The New Yorker* in 2016, " 'The Communist Manifesto' is like a bomb about to go off in your hands."[34] Indeed. It is hard to read the *Manifesto* in 2018 without feeling its continuing, angry influence all around.

One sphere where Marxism continues to enjoy prominence is in the Ivory Tower. It is an exaggeration to say that American academics are mostly Marxists—as an academic myself, I know very few professors who would call themselves Marxist. (Please don't all reach out at once.) Yet broadly, Marxist habits of speech and mind have firmly lodged themselves in the vernacular of academic discourse. Much of the currently fashionable catchphrases of academia—postcolonialism, neoliberalism, hierarchy, social justice—often betray a set of assumptions resonating with Marx: that the story of Western history is one of economic materialism, class oppression, false consciousness, and group opposition. Although Marxist purists deride contemporary identity politics as bad for proletarian cohesion, the pervasive impulse to define one's identity and political standing by reference to an "oppressed" class comes straight from Marx and Engels's playbook.

Marxism also enjoys hipster status in popular culture. Young people aren't too attracted to the portly image of Marx, but the stern, charismatic face of Argentine Marxist revolutionary Che Guevara adorns countless t-shirts and banners around college campuses and trendy coffee houses. Never mind that Guevara was responsible for the murder of countless Christians and other innocents, or that he proclaimed "I am not Christ or a philanthropist, old lady, I am all the contrary of a Christ," and "If Christ himself stood in my way, I, like Nietzsche, would not hesitate to squish him like a worm." Popular culture wants romantic counterculture, and Marxist icons fill the need.

And then one can wonder whether Marxism might still make a political comeback, even in seemingly inhospitable places such as the United States. In 2016, the Victims of Communism Memorial Foundation released a report on contemporary attitudes toward Communism in the United States.[35] Among other things, it found that just

37 percent of Millennials and 38 percent of Generation Z have an unfavorable attitude toward Communism, 25 percent had a favorable opinion of Lenin, nearly a third of all Millennials believed that George Bush killed more people than Joseph Stalin (Stalin's genocides killed around 20 million people), and 64 percent of Americans agreed with the classic Karl Marx statement: "From each according to his abilities, to each according to his needs." As this book is being written, the Venezuelan government is attempting to put these ideas into practice. The United States won't be next, but could it be down the road?

Despite the history of the late twentieth century, the ideas Marx and Engels proposed in the *Communist Manifesto* still have legs. Marx once argued that, since religion was a human creation stemming from oppressive economic conditions, one could expect that once Communism abolished those economic conditions, then religion would naturally fade.[36] That self-serving prophesy has been falsified by history. But it would be equally wrongheaded to claim that Marxism will naturally fade along with the nineteenth-century economic conditions that prompted it. Though rooted in a particular time and place, Marx advanced a powerful historical, economic, social, and political vision that has spoken to hearts and minds across time and place. Now, as much as ever, the church needs to understand Marx's arguments, take them seriously, and offer a measured response—one that engages without demonizing and offers not just refutations but thoughtful, practical solutions.

Oh, and as to the question of seeing God in space, there is a wonderful story (which may be apocryphal) about a Soviet teacher gloating to his class that Yuri Gagarin had looked around and didn't see God. A little girl then inquires whether the cosmonaut had a pure heart. The teacher is mystified until the girl quotes the Beatitude, "Blessed are the pure in heart, for they shall see God" (Matt. 5:8). Touché. As much as Marxism needs a response from the mind, it needs responses from the heart even more.

CHAPTER 6

Sigmund Freud's Ego and
The Future of an Illusion

*"All [religious doctrines] are illusions—indemonstrable—and
no one can be forced to hold them true, to believe in them."*

Sigmund Freud
The Future of an Illusion (1927)

On the night of May 10, 1933, a group of forty thousand angry
university students gathered in a European capital's public square
to destroy a collection of unwholesome books. The students eagerly
unloaded the condemned volumes from trucks, waved them deri-
sively in the air, and then cast them into a gargantuan bonfire blaz-
ing in the center of the square. As the flames licked the night skies,
a spiritual leader gave an impassioned speech, exhorting the crowd
to rid themselves of the moral filth and perversion contained in the
assembled books. By the night's end, twenty thousand volumes of offensive works had been burned to ashes.

Among the many authors targeted that night, one stood out as
a flagrant symbol of twentieth-century intellectual decay and degen-
eracy. The author was still alive and residing in an adjacent country,
although the forces at work at the book burning would soon bring
his life into mortal peril. For now, the students were just burning his
books, but they made it quite clear that they might just as well burn
the man himself. As they torched his works, the students chanted:
"Against the soul-destroying overestimation of the sex life—and on
behalf of the nobility of the human soul, we offer to the flames the
writings of Sigmund Freud."[1]

This time, the censor was not the church. The place was the Be-
belplatz in Berlin, the capital of Germany, and its once and future
intellectual heart. The censor was the National Socialist or Nazi Party,
newly ascendant in German politics. The students were joined by

brown-shirted storm troopers; and the spiritual leader giving the speech was Nazi propaganda minister Joseph Goebbels, who wanted to replace Christianity with a pagan civil religion centered on the German people and the state. Many other authors' works deemed "anti-German" went up in flames that night, including Albert Einstein, Ernest Hemingway, Helen Keller, Jack London, Thomas Mann, Karl Marx, Marcel Proust, Upton Sinclair, and H. G. Wells. It was the beginning of the Nazi intellectual purge and its relentless march toward war and Holocaust.

Even though the church was not the culprit in the book burning and soon incurred its own oppression from the Nazis, many Christians in Europe and America had similarly strong misgivings about Sigmund Freud. Many Christians shared the Nazis' view that Freud's theory of dreams and the subconscious and his psychoanalytic methods overestimated and perverted the role of sex in human psychology and gravely threatened the moral order. Indeed, many conservative Christians in the early decades of the twentieth century found Freud's growing influence nearly as threatening as Hitler's.

Nor did Freud give offense to Christians only indirectly or, like Darwin, make an effort to find common ground. To the contrary, Freud reveled in provocation, repeatedly drawing on his work on the psychology and the human unconscious to expose religion as a fraud. It was in 1927, in his *The Future of an Illusion*, that Freud made his claim most explicitly: Religion is an illusion, a wish fulfillment, created by society for the purpose of mediating civilization's cruel edges. Religion provides the illusory comfort that, after infancy, there is still a father figure to protect us. It was time for society to grow up from this infantile thinking, Freud argued, to grow up and move on to rationalist maturity.

The Future of an Illusion seemed to validate the predictions that many Christians had been making since Freud's views on the human psyche had been popularized decades earlier: Freudianism was rank atheism, an assault on God, Christendom, and the very foundations of morality and society. Along with Darwin and Marx, Freud filled out a satanic troika whose influence had to be arrested at all costs.

But the fact that the Nazis—surely as great antagonists of true Christianity as ever existed—reacted to Freud with such venom might give us some pause. Does the ancient Sanskrit proverb "the enemy of my enemy is my friend" have any resonance for the church? A man who called the Christian religion an illusion couldn't exactly be counted a friend, but perhaps we could listen critically to his message rather than attack his books?

Perhaps more than any other book we have examined, Sigmund Freud's work produced a wide variety of conflicting reactions from the church. Freud's theories split the human mind into opposing forces. His depiction of human nature and its relationship to the divine split the church into opposing factions. Some were furious and hateful. Others were sympathetic or even fawningly sycophantic. Some Christians saw in Freud the antichrist, others saw in him an unknowing follower of Christ and a benevolent shepherd for the mentally afflicted. In between these poles, Christian thinkers in the twentieth century and beyond have tended to be wary in reacting to Freud. But react to him they must, for Freud rocked the entire modern age: the church, the world, and all.

IN HIS FATHER'S SHADOW

Sigismund Schlomo Freud was born to Orthodox Jewish parents in Moravia—current-day Czech Republic—in 1856. In young adulthood, he dropped the "Schlomo" and the "is" in Sigismund and became Sigmund Freud, the name by which the entire Western world would soon come to know him.

Given the field of psychoanalysis that Freud pioneered and its emphasis on the permanent impact of childhood development, any narration of his personal biography instinctively links the significant events in his life to his subsequent intellectual theories. Thus, for example, one cannot study Freud's theory of a pervasive Oedipus complex—the theory that children become infatuated with their parent of the opposite sex and look at their parent of the same sex as a rival for the opposite-sex parent's affection—without noticing that Freud had an elderly father who married a woman less than half his age and half-brothers who were almost his mother's age. Similarly, that Freud's father, a struggling wool merchant, was a poor financial provider and appeared as less than manly in standing up to the pervasive anti-Semitism of nineteenth-century Austro-Hungary may have colored Freud's dramatic claims about father-son relationships and the nature of God as a father.

But there was one relationship early in Freud's life that stands out as potentially most significant in understanding his subsequent, sometimes ambivalent, hostility to religion. During his early formative years—the years Freud would subsequently identify as critical in a person's psychological development—a Roman Catholic nursemaid took care of Freud while his mother attended to a sickly brother. The nursemaid took young Sigmund to church and indoctrinated him in Catholic theology. Then she was abruptly dismissed on accusations of theft, leaving Freud bereft of an early religious mother figure. Some scholars have argued that Freud's subsequent hostility to Christianity grew out of his feeling of abandonment by an important religious influence at an impressionable time of his life. However lasting this influence may have been, Freud remained infatuated with the City of Rome and certain Christian holidays, such as Easter, for the rest of his life.

After the nursemaid's departure, Freud's religious education at home was limited. Although his father was only modestly observant of Jewish holidays, he did read the Bible aloud in Hebrew. In 1860 his family moved to Vienna—the city with which Freud would become permanently associated—where Freud received a more rigorous Jewish education. At the age of seventeen, he enrolled at the University of Vienna and studied under the distinguished philosopher Franz Brentano, who had left the Catholic priesthood because he rejected the pope's claim to infallibility. Brentano exposed Freud to a broad, liberal education and, at one point, apparently came near to persuading him to become a believer on the strength of rational argument. Freud admitted to finding Brentano's arguments compelling, but he ultimately rejected them and gravitated to other intellectual influences. Particularly influential in the development of Freud's eventual critical view of religion was the philosopher Ludwig Feuerbach, who was nominally a believer but whose book *The Essence of Christianity* argued that religion is simply the projection of deep-seated human needs—that Christianity's claim to divine truth was, in effect, "an illusion."

At the same time that he was developing atheistic convictions, Freud began to develop a set of professional skills that would propel him to fame. Working with a group of psychologists, Freud began to search for causes of psychological phenomena on purely material grounds. Rejecting spiritualistic accounts of human thoughts, attitudes, and mental illnesses, Freud worked toward understanding psychology as a scientific and medical discipline, thus helping to create the medical discipline of psychiatry.

In 1886, on Easter Sunday, Freud opened a private practice in neuropathology. In that profession, he would transition away from prevailing treatment methods involving hypnosis and perfect his techniques of psychoanalysis: the therapeutic system that aims to treat mental disorders by investigating the interaction of conscious and unconscious mental elements, and bringing repressed conflicts, fears, and desires into the conscious mind by methods such as dream interpretation and free association. His practice afforded Freud sufficient income to marry and support a family, but the position he most coveted was a professorship at the University of Vienna. That position was long denied him due to Austrian anti-Semitism, and it took pulling strings with a politically connected former patient to help him finally secure a professorial position in 1902.

The combination of a clinical practice with many interesting cases on which to draw and a prestigious academic appointment afforded Freud the platform to launch his revolutionary academic work. In 1899, his first published work to receive wide attention—although sales were slow at first—was *The Interpretation of Dreams*. It was in this book that Freud rolled out a new theory of the human unconscious, as revealed in dreams. All dreams, Freud argued, are wish fulfillments. Because the background information compiled in the unconscious is often disorganized and disturbing, the mind "censors" the content and only permits it to pass into the dream in a disguised or symbolic form. Hence, as Freud would further discuss in later work, dream symbolism would become critical to dream interpretation, and hence a key to understanding the human unconscious and its many behavioral manifestations.

Totem and Taboo, published in 1913, applied Freud's psychoanalytic theories to archaeology, anthropology, and religion. In the fourth chapter of *Totem*, Freud staked a claim, subsequently made famous, that would become central to his subsequent work on religion. Drawing on Darwin's theory that early human communities centered on a powerful alpha male surrounded by a harem of females, Freud argued that totemism—the construction of sacred symbolic objects such as idols—had its origins in a concrete historical fact. Freud speculated that a band of prehistoric brothers expelled by their father from the harem-group returned to kill their father, whom they simultaneously feared and respected. Freud thus located the origins of the previously described Oedipus complex in the cradle of human civilization and postulated that all religion was the manifestation of collective guilt and ambivalence over the murder of the primeval father figure.

As Freud's international reputation grew and psychoanalysis became widely known, Freud found it increasingly difficult to maintain intellectual loyalty among his disciples. During the second decade of the twentieth century, Freud saw a number of his prominent supporters and collaborators abandon his organization—the International Psychoanalytical Association—and develop their own theories. Most famous of the defectors was Carl Jung, the Swiss psychiatrist who broke with Freud over a number of issues, including the importance of sexual motivation in human psychology. Jung argued that Freud overrated the importance of sex, a point that Freud vehemently denied.

Much of Freud's early work centered on claims that human behavior principally arose from sexual instincts: *eros* or *libido*. As we shall see, the sexually explicit and often morally shocking nature of Freud's interpretations earned him sharp criticisms in many quarters. But in 1920, in *Beyond the Pleasure Principle*, Freud shifted his emphasis and introduced the idea of the "death wish" as another strong and competing human motivation. Though the erotic impulse propels a person toward reproduction and self-preservation, the death wish—the biological pressure on cells to return to their inanimate state manifested throughout the human body and psyche—exerts an opposite impulse to bring about death.

This idea of human psychology as torn between equal and opposite impulses led Freud to publish his most important and enduring idea in *The Ego and the Id* in 1923. There, Freud argued that all human psychology can be understood as the conflict between opposed internal forces—the ego (the rational and mediating agency of the mind) against the id (the forces of the mind governed by uncoordinated instinct), the ego against the superego (the critical and moral agency of the mind), and the erotic impulse against the death wish. The ideas that came together in *Ego* were revolutionary in psychology because they shattered the conventional mind/body dualism that had prevailed in Western thought since classical times, and asserted that the human mind was a much more complex and internally conflicted organ than Enlightenment rationalism had allowed. Freud thus became associated with nineteenth-century Romanticism, a movement that predated him by half a century. The human mind wasn't simply a rational computer fighting to keep in check the body's animal instincts. The mind itself was split and internally contending, much like Robert Louis Stevenson's Dr. Jekyll and Mr. Hyde.

Perhaps if Freud had been a more superstitious man he would have come to believe in the cruelty of fate. For in the same year that Freud published his most important work, *Ego,* he was diagnosed with cancer of the jaw, a consequence of decades of heavy smoking. Surgeons removed the upper part of his palate, and Freud was given a painful and poorly fitting prosthesis. Freud continued his life's work, but in the shadow of chronic pain.

In the late 1920s, perhaps motivated by reflections on the brutal culmination of the First World War, Freud's scholarly work took a turn from the inner mind to the outward manifestations of culture. In 1927, he published *The Future of an Illusion,* his most complete and direct critique of religion, which we shall examine in greater detail momentarily. He followed up in 1929 with *Civilization and its Discontents,* another one of his most important works, in which Freud sketched out the inherent tension between society and the individual. According to Freud, individuals possess an immutable predisposition to satisfy sexual urges and engage in violence against authority figures and sexual competitors, and civilization must constantly suppress these desires and harshly punish their exercise, thereby creating perpetual tension.

Social tension was surely in the air as Freud penned these words, with the plunge into global economic depression and the rising specter of Fascism in the Germanic world. For Freud, a Jew, the rise of Nazism was particularly alarming, and the events of 1933 revealed the growing personal threat on his doorstep. Following the Nazi book burning, Freud quipped: "What progress we are making. In the Middle Ages they would have burned me. Now, they are content with burning my books."[2] Despite his danger, Freud initially resisted the impulse to immigrate to a safer location. Even after the Nazis invaded Austria in March 1938, putting Freud and his family into grave danger, he wanted to stay. By late 1938, however, the situation had become untenable. Freud and his family eventually managed to escape Vienna with the help of Princess Marie Bonaparte and the government of the United States (which he despised due to America's excessive materialism), with President Roosevelt taking a personal interest in his case. The Nazis made Freud's emigration contingent on him signing a statement saying that he had not been molested and, indeed, had been allowed to continue his scientific work. Freud added a sarcastic coda: "I can most highly recommend the Gestapo to everyone." (In a twist of historical irony, it was recently discovered that a picture of a church that Hitler painted while a young struggling artist may once have hung in Freud's medical office.)

Settled in London and continuing to battle his painful cancer, Freud completed his final book, *Moses and Monotheism*, in 1939. Signaling an evolving and less hostile stance toward religion—at least Judaism—Freud argued that Judaism actually marked cultural progress by freeing humanity from the strictures of the empirical world and opening up fresh possibilities for contemplation and introspection. Because the Jews worshipped an invisible God ("Thou shalt not make any graven image"), Freud argued, their minds were opened up to abstraction and they were able exalt "intellectuality over sensuality," a transition that paved the way for the rationalistic tradition in Western civilization. The book also included some bizarre interpretations of the Jewish faith. Consistent with the psychological phenomenon of inversion, Freud asserted that Moses was actually an Egyptian rather than an Israelite, that the Israelites had rescued him from the Nile rather than the other way around, that monotheism was an Egyptian rather than Jewish creation, originating in the Egyptian cult of the sun god Aten, and that the Jews had murdered Moses.

For a time, it seemed that *Moses and Monotheism* might not ever see its way to print. Prominent Jewish Londoners lobbied Freud not to publish the book, arguing that the Jews had enough trouble without one of their own claiming that the Jews had actually murdered the Egyptian Moses. Freud disregarded their entreaties and published the book anyway in German and in English. Amid nasty reviews but strong sales figures, Freud thumbed his nose at the world and endorsed his own book as "quite a worthy exit."

Later that year, Freud suffered increasing torment in his jaw. When his doctors declared it inoperable, he asked them to help him terminate his life, and they obliged. On September 23, 1939, following the administration of large quantities of morphine, Sigmund Freud passed from this world, his euthanasia adding a sad ending to an already controversial life.

ILLUSIONS AND DELUSIONS

As we have seen, the philosopher Feuerbach—who so influenced young Sigmund Freud—argued that religion is an "illusion." In *The Future of an Illusion,* Freud took up this theme and developed it into a comprehensive argument, grounded in the psychoanalytic method, against religious belief.

Freud's argument begins with the key concept of culture (or civilization—Freud refused any distinction between the two). Culture comes into place to solve economic and social problems and to defend humanity against nature. Though it is necessary to human survival, culture also imposes hardships on individuals by limiting their freedom to fulfill their desires. The imposition of culture thus engenders resentment against culture. According to Freud, culture creates religion as a means of mediating these resentments and ensuring its own survival.

If the survival of culture is religion's raison d'être, then what explains the particular form of religion: the attachment to the idea of a powerful Father God? Here, Freud reverts to his earlier arguments about child psychological development. "The mother, who satisfies the child's hunger, becomes the first love-object and certainly the first protection against all the vague, threatening dangers of the external world."[3] Eventually, however, the stronger father takes the mother's place as prime protector, and the child transfers onto the father his ambivalent feelings of respect and jealousy. To Freud, belief in a Father God was a projection of infantile desires for paternal protection in the face of a hostile world.

But why would society perpetuate a belief in divine paternal protection in the absence of evidence of God's existence? Here, it is important to understand Freud's choice to describe religion as an "illusion." Illusions, Freud argued, differ from errors. For example, Aristotle's belief that vermin spontaneously generate from filth is, to Freud, an example of a simple error. Religion, on the other hand, is akin to Columbus's belief that he had discovered a new sea route to India. Columbus wanted to find India and hence insisted on imposing the framework of his wishes on the physical evidence he discovered upon reaching North America. In the same way, Freud argued, religion acts as a wish fulfillment. People desperately desire protection from the world's cruel vagaries, and hence they construct complex fictions—religion—in order to satisfy their wishes: "Through the kind rule of divine Providence, anxiety over the dangers of life is assuaged; the introduction of a moral world order ensures the fulfillment of the demand for justice, so often unmet in human society" (93). Religion was thus akin to a dream—an unfulfilled desire filtered by the unconscious mind into concrete symbolic images.

Freud anticipated the social criticisms that would inevitably be levied against his arguments. Wasn't it the case that, throughout history, religion had served the salutary cultural function of preserving order in society and that abolishing it would plunge society into chaos? And wouldn't dispelling religious illusion be a severe cruelty to the "countless people [who] find their only comfort in the doctrines of religion, and can endure life only with the help of those doctrines?" (96). Freud pled not guilty to these charges, asserting that he would be the only one harmed by the publication of his book, because of the unfair accusations that would be leveled against him. As for others, the book's publication would be benign. Psychoanalysis might be attacked on the ground that *Illusion* revealed it to lead to atheism, but the discipline had already weathered many storms, and proponents of religion could easily turn psychoanalysis to their own causes. More generally, Freud protested that he was certainly not the first to demonstrate religion's delusional character: "Criticism has eaten away at the evidential force of religious documents, natural science has exposed the errors contained therein, and comparative research has noticed the fatal resemblance between the religious ideas we revere and the mental products of primitive peoples and times" (99). Given that people already had a growing number of reasons not to believe in God, it would be better for society to help them dispense with religious ideas and replace them with other sources of morality.

Allowing them to drift along with slowly eroding belief was the real danger: "If the only reason one must not kill one's neighbor is that God has forbidden it and will exact a severe punishment for it in this life or the next, and if one then learns that there is no God and that one need not fear his punishment, then one will certainly kill one's neighbors without qualms" (100).

Freud allowed that there was some historical truth to religion, in the limited sense in which religions represent a taboo against patricide in reaction to the historical fact (in Freud's view, expressed in *Totem and Taboo*) of the killing of primal father and subsequent guilt and prohibition against killing. Although this ancient history might lend metaphorical truth to religious systems, the religious systems had grown so attenuated from the underlying historical facts as to be no more true than a parent's claim that storks bring the baby—a metaphorical fairy tale that so distorts the truth that its earlier telling engenders mistrust when the child eventually learns the truth.

Finally, Freud turned to the possibility that he himself was subject to an illusion—that his arguments against the existence of God were simply wish fulfillments, just like arguments for the existence of God. Freud demurred on methodological grounds. His God was *Logos*, or Reason, or scientific method. If subsequent scientific inquiry demonstrated the particulars of Freud's claims to be incorrect and replaced them with others, this would not then demonstrate that Freud had been subject to an illusion, only that his knowledge had been incomplete. Science, to Freud, is a process rather than an end: "Transformations of scientific opinion are developments, progress— not the overthrow of the old order" (113).

Some scholars regard *Illusion* as strikingly out of step with the corpus of Freud's work, as "a throwback to eighteenth century critiques of religion, a redux of Enlightenment values in the twentieth century."[4] By asserting that only empirically derived knowledge is real, *Illusion* calls into doubt the thrust of Freud's work on the subconscious and keeps more intellectual company with the eighteenth-century rationalist *philosophes* than with twentieth-century Romantics. Upon its initial publication, *Illusion* received decidedly mixed reviews, with some defenders but many critics. Typical were the comments of the poet T. S. Eliot, who found the book "shrewd yet stupid" for its vague use of terminology and circular definition of "illusion." Freud himself offered his own work a surprisingly negative assessment: "This is my worst book! It isn't a book of Freud. It's the book of an old man."[5] Whether he was being self-deprecating or actually believed this is . . . open to analysis.

Popular media accounts of the book's publication played up its atheism to inflammatory effect. A December 1927 *New York Times* headline read: "Religion Doomed / Freud Asserts / Says It Is at Point Where It Must Give Way Before Science / His Followers Chagrined / Master Psychoanalyst's New Book Deplored Dissention It is Expected to Cause."[6] Although this headline overstated the defection rate among Freud's disciples, the book's publication certainly did send shockwaves throughout the West. Freud, by then the undisputed psychiatric grandmaster of the twentieth century, claimed that religion was rightly on its way out.

How *Illusion* Rocked the Church

It is not difficult to understand how a book claiming that all religion—the Christian religion in particular—is an illusion would cause offense and difficulty to the church. But, beyond the headline of the book's title, it is worth spending a moment on the different levels of argument and implications for Christians presented in *The Future of an Illusion*. They are not all obvious or simple to rebut.

First, *Illusion* advanced a naturalistic explanation for the formation and persistence of religious belief. A conventional argument for the existence of God is the universal human belief in God. Why would men and women across time and place come up with, and cling to, beliefs in God unless there was some basis for that belief? For example, the French mathematician and theologian Blaise Pascal argued in his *Pensées* that there is a God-shaped vacuum in the heart of every person, and it can never be filled by any created thing. It can only be filled by God, made known through Jesus Christ. In *Illusion*, Freud disputed this assertion. Not only was religious belief misguided, but it could also be explained in concrete historical and psychological terms as a pathological reaction to the assassination of an actual father figure and the persistent insecurity that such a treasonous act would create. Although Freud could not prove the historical fact of the father-figure murder, *Illusion* framed its argument on the authority of Freud's decades of clinical experience with psychoanalysis. It was as if Freud were saying, "I've seen hundreds of cases just like yours. I can tell with certainty where your misguided beliefs come from because I've seen it all before."

Second, Freud argued that belief in God was not merely misguided, but also a kind of deluded wishful thinking that led to bad social outcomes. Social thinkers, even those skeptical of Christianity's claims to historical truth (such as some of the American founding fathers), had long described religion as a form of salutary social control useful in forming group cohesion, controlling selfish and destructive behavior, and creating allegiance to the state. Freud, however, treated religion as a psychiatric pathology, the kind of mental illness he would have treated in his patients as they reclined on a couch. After all, the whole point of psychotherapy was to unmask the patient's subconscious wishes that had become disguised—that is, illusions—in dreams, "Freudian slips," and neurotic behaviors. All this so that his patients, having seen their wishes uncloaked, could heal themselves. *Illusion* essentially offered social group therapy, inviting society at large to heal itself of its collective and problematic illusions by unmasking the suppressed wishes that religious symbolism concealed.

Finally, *Illusion* offered society and individuals a motivation to move on from religion. Ambivalent attachment to a father figure was natural in the infantile stage of an individual and perhaps in society as well. But the persistence of that belief long after the children outgrew their physical fathers as both protector and rival was inconsistent with maturation and adulthood. It was infantile. Therefore, religion was infantile. There are few tactics more effective than telling someone that they need to grow up, that their beliefs or actions are those of children. The apostle Paul repeatedly used this tactic: for example, observing in 1 Corinthians 13:11 that, although he once thought and reasoned like a child, when he grew up and became a man, he put off childish things. *And so should you, people of Corinth.*

Although each of these angles to Freud's arguments creates direct challenges to Christian theology and practice, there are also important aspects in which each argument actually resonates with Christian teachings in ways that Freud may not have anticipated or intended. In a moment, we will hear directly from some eminent Christian thinkers who engaged sympathetically with Freud. But for now, a brief rejoinder—or perhaps redirection—of each of Freud's points.

First, Freud's explanation of the origins of religion is not far afield from the Christian explanation for the origins of idolatry. Think of the story of the people of Israel and the golden calf (Exod. 32). When Moses had been away a long time on Mount Sinai, the people began to grow restless and demanded the creation of an idol that would take the place of their true Father and fulfill their wish for protection and provision ("a god who will go before us"; Exod. 32:1). Bulls or calves were pervasive religious symbols in the Middle East, often associated with the strength and courage of the king—the father protector. From a biblical perspective, then, Freud's interpretation of the psychological origins of *false* religions seems uncontroversial, even illuminating. Certainly, Freud would not have accepted a Christian anti-idolatry interpretation as a friendly amendment to his theories, but so what? A theory presented as hostile that, with amendment, becomes sympathetic is still a useful theory.

Second, the idea of religious dogma as harmful to the body and soul is not anathema to the Christian. Indeed, much of Jesus' ministry was devoted to breaking the stranglehold of life-denying pharisaical religion. Recall the Savior's harsh words in Matthew 23:15: "Woe to you, teachers of the law and Pharisees, you hypocrites! You travel over land and sea to win a single convert, and when you have succeeded, you make them twice as much a child of hell as you are." Over and over, Jesus made it clear that he had come to heal the sick, those oppressed by sin and held in bondage by an inflexible, performance-based religion. By emphasizing the spirit of the law over legal rules, Jesus asserted that, like Freud, he was no defender of conventional religion and would readily have agreed that much of it is deeply pathological.

Finally, Jesus would have taken no exception to Freud's claim that Christianity is infantile. To the contrary, Jesus told Nicodemus that he would have to be born again to enter the kingdom of heaven (John 3:5–8). Later, he told his disciples that unless they entered the kingdom of heaven as little children, they would not enter at all (Matt. 18:3), and told them to call God "Abba" or Daddy (Mark 14:36).

Throughout the New Testament, the Christian faith is presented as a story of radical inversion: the first is last, poor is rich, weakness is strength, foolishness is wisdom, and infancy is maturity. It would take a much longer chapter to ponder the meaning of this; for now, however, it is enough to observe that Freud's charges of infantilism could well be greeted by the Christian with an innocent thank-you.

DIRTY OLD MAN OR WORTHY INTERLOCUTOR?

As he surely intended, Freud's work in general, and *Illusion* in particular, caught the attention of Christians around the world. Sometimes, the church's reaction was respectful and engaged. At other times, it was virulent, mean-spirited, and even racist. The church was rocked, sometimes in one direction, sometimes in another.

An early example of constructive dialogue between Freud and the church occurred in the correspondence between Freud and Oskar Pfister, a Lutheran pastor in Zurich, Switzerland, immediately following *Illusion*'s publication. Pfister had been practicing psychoanalysis with his parishioners, particularly young adults, since 1909 and was a great admirer of Freud. Pfister and Freud met in the early 1920s, and Freud became particularly indebted to Pfister when the pastor took Freud's side against Pfister's fellow countryman Jung. Freud and Pfister engaged in cordial correspondence about *Illusion* and, with Freud's encouragement, Pfister published a response, *The Illusion of a Future*, in 1928 in Freud's own magazine. While maintaining a sympathetic tone to Freud's larger project, however, Pfister chided Freud for an excessively empiricist approach to truth: an approach that ignored the importance of intuition and sensation, which even rationalists such as John Stuart Mill had embraced. Further, Pfister argued that Freud had failed to understand the evolutionary progress in religion: how it had outgrown its primitive state of neurosis and infantilism, which Freud still attributed to it, and had grown into a mature system of thought and practice that stood as a bulwark against evil in the modern world. In an appeal designed to underline his loyalty to Freud's broader project, Pfister argued that psychoanalysis had actually begun with Jesus, who healed a lame man "from within," who understood the psychic reality of demons, and who handled transference as loving attachment to "absolute, ideal achievements so that no new attachments ensue."[7]

In his private correspondence with Freud, Pfister went even further, suggesting that Freud was performing a greater service for Christ than most Christians. Pfister related Freud to Jesus' parable of the two sons (Matt. 21:28–31), one of whom verbally refused to work in the vineyard but eventually did, and the other who compliantly agreed to work in the vineyard but never did. Pfister compared Freud to the first son, whom the parable taught had actually done God's will:

> Will you be angry with me for seeing you, who caught such glorious rays of the eternal light and consumed yourself in the struggle for truth and human love, as figuratively closer to the throne of God, despite your supposed lack of belief, than many a churchman who mumbles prayers and performs ceremonies, but whose heart never shone with understanding and good will toward man? And since for the Gospel-oriented Christian everything depends on doing the divine will and not on saying "Lord! Lord!," do you understand how even I could envy you?[8]

Regrettably, much of the response to *Illusion* from European Christendom lacked Pfister's thoughtfulness and instead reeked of anti-Semitism. Carl Christian Clemen, a professor of ethnology at the University of Bonn, took the occasion of *Illusion*'s publication to relate psychoanalysis's sexual emphasis to Freud's ethnicity, impugning Jewish people with pervasive sexual depravity.[9] Racist ad hominem attacks flew from many other quarters as well, as distinguished German intellectuals wondered how it was that Jews felt themselves authorized "to offer a judgment on the Christian faith."[10] Christian anti-Freud rhetoric heated up even further after the publication of *Moses and Monotheism*. Catholic writers, who found the book "unquotable," wondered whether Freud had "a sexual obsession" and called for his expulsion from England.[11] Outraged readers from around the world unloaded abuse on Freud, much of it virulently anti-Semitic.

Early on, Freud was surprisingly well received in America, despite America's reputation in Europe for Puritan prudishness. During a 1909 trip to the United States, Freud found himself better treated than he ever had been on the Continent: "In Europe I felt as though I were despised but in America I found myself received by the foremost of men as an equal."[12] His reception was particularly favorable among mainstream Protestant churches, which incorporated Freudian principles into pastoral counseling techniques, and among faith-healing movements on the fringe of Christendom such as Christian Science.

Following the Fundamentalist-Modernist split in in American churches in the 1920s, however, Freud became widely abused in fundamentalist circles. Many dismissed him as a dirty old man and viewed his critical views on religion as merely the logical outgrowth of his sick moral character. To conservative Christians, Freud's perseveration with sexual explanations for psychological attributes was "crude and degrading."[13] Many Christians considered Freud's theories too prurient even to discuss. In 1930, the director of religious education for the Presbyterian Church asserted: "If I should explain what [Freud's] theories are and this article were published in the *Presbyterian*, the publishers would lay [*sic*] themselves liable for fine and imprisonment for sending obscene literature through the mails."[14] William Newell, of the Moody Bible Institute in Chicago, expressed his disgust with "rotten Freud's" teachings as "hog-sty doctrines" of wickedness, equating them with Darwin's teaching that man came from monkeys.[15]

The pairing of Freud with Darwin was a common rhetorical move among conservative Christian critics. A 1930 editorial titled "The Freudian Menace in the King's Business," in the monthly newsletter of The Bible Institute of Los Angeles (now Biola University), warned that "a more subtle and dangerous foe to the Church than evolution has been will yet be found in the sphere of psychology." While evolution dealt only with the origins of life, Freudian psychology "strikes indirectly at the foundation of the Christian faith" by denying and displacing "every idea of moral obligation to God and man."[16] Most conservative American Christians saw no possibility that Freud's work in psychotherapy and research on the operation of the mind could be salvaged, even in part, after his atheistic claims in *Illusion* and other works. Freudianism was a single, unified package of perdition.

Some prominent Christian intellectuals and theologians engaged more sympathetically with Freud's critiques of religion and his wider project in psychology and philosophy. A position common to a number of leading mid-twentieth-century Christians was that much of Freud's work—particularly the clinical aspects—could be accepted without buying into his philosophical claims. In *Mere Christianity*, C. S. Lewis argued as much:

> When Freud is talking about how to cure neurotics he is speaking as a specialist on his own subject, but when he goes on to talk general philosophy he is speaking as an amateur. . . . But psychoanalysis itself, apart from all the philosophical additions that Freud and others have made to it, is not in the least contradictory to Christianity.[17]

The liberal theologian Paul Tillich similarly asserted that "it would be wrong to refuse to listen to what Freud said about *psychological reality*, simply because we know in advance that we will not agree with some of his philosophical conclusions about *ultimate reality*."[18] Though Tillich rejected Freud's atheistic conclusions, he found that Freud's views more generally contained much material of great interest to Christian theology.

Similarly, the eminent American theologian Reinhold Niebuhr engaged Freud with interest and collegiality, finding Freud's work a welcome counterpoint to anti-Christian assumptions of Enlightenment thinking.[19] Although recognizing that Freud was not interested in traditional Christian doctrines, Niebuhr argued that Freud "broke open the optimism of the Enlightenment" with respect to innate human goodness and hence supported the more pessimistic Christian conception of human dispositions and morality.[20] Whereas Enlightenment thinkers had embraced a dualistic mind-body conception and assumed that if the mind could be sufficiently disciplined to conquer the body human happiness would result, Freud's theories about the mind divided into competing components—id, ego, and superego—shattered such grounds for optimism. In so doing, Freud aligned modern psychology with traditional Christian pessimism about human nature grounded in the doctrine of original sin. Where Freud erred, argued Niebuhr, was in adopting an excessively naturalistic theory of the mind that failed to "do full justice to the transcendent freedom of spirit of which the self is capable and . . . the creative and destructive possibilities of that freedom."[21]

In more recent years, prominent Christian psychologists have stressed the need for Christians to engage seriously and respectfully with Freud's ideas. In 1987, Dan Blazer, the dean of Medical Education at Duke University Medical School, wrote *Freud vs. God: How Psychiatry Lost Its Soul and Christianity Lost Its Mind*. As the provocative title suggests, Blazer argued that the psychiatric profession had lost its grip on the soul—the deeper aspects of meaning and community that animate all genuine human life—and evangelical Christianity, by unthinkingly embracing the worst aspects of psychiatry, had lost a genuinely Christian understanding of the mind. Blazer prescribed continuing, engaged dialogue between Freudian and Christian worldviews as necessary for psychiatry to reclaim its soul and Christianity its mind.

For many years, Dr. Armand Nicholi, a professor of psychiatry at Harvard Medical School and a Christian, taught a course contrasting the views of Sigmund Freud and C. S. Lewis on profound issues such as happiness, sex, love, pain, and death. In 2002, Nicholi published a widely discussed book—*C. S. Lewis and Sigmund Freud Debate God, Love, Sex, and the Meaning of Life*—that traced the two men's biographies in parallel, and compared and contrasted their views on these and other topics. Nicholi makes the tantalizing suggestion, based on historical records, that Lewis may have visited Freud in London during the fifteen months before Freud's death. He posits that the respective titans of atheism and Christianity engaged in a cordial social and intellectual exchange. Whether that confab actually occurred is perhaps less important than the fact that it *could have occurred*. To imagine a figure as revered by contemporary Christians as C. S. Lewis eagerly and respectfully engaging with Sigmund Freud—searching for common ground, earnestly probing differences, ending the rendezvous with good-faith pledges of continued mutual deliberation—casts the Christian view on Freud as necessarily other than the "hog-sty doctrines of wickedness" perspective.

Despite these and other Christian efforts to engage Freud respectfully and even sympathetically, the "dirty old man" perspective remains prominent too. Many Christians continue to roll their eyes to either heaven (summoning aid) or hell (scanning for the man) at the mention of Freud's name. Particularly in light of the sexual revolution of the late twentieth century, Freud has come under heavy fire as the original libertine instigator. For example, Albert Mohler, president of the Southern Baptist Theological Seminary, pins the increasing social acceptance of pornography on Freudian thinking, arguing that "the doctrine of sin explains why we have exchanged the glory of God for Sigmund Freud's concept of polymorphous perversity."[22] Many Christians continue to associate Freud with lewdness, moral corruption, and bitter atheism.

The church has not made its peace with Sigmund Freud; it probably never will. And perhaps Freud would have wanted it that way.

THE FUTURE OF SIGMUND FREUD

How have Freud's theories, and Freudianism more broadly, weathered the passage of the seven decades since his death? At one level, Freud likely would be disappointed to learn that many of the particulars of his theories and techniques have been rejected by modern psychology. Many scholars consider the Freudian system functionally obsolete. A good number of Freud's explanations for psychological phenomena, including many of the seemingly bizarre and prurient sexual explanations that so shocked and offended people when they were first publicized and haven't really mellowed over time, have been dismissed by later scientific inquiry as groundless and speculative. For example, precious little evidence exists to support Freud's conjecture of a pervasive Oedipus complex—that boys love their mothers and hate their fathers. Harvard cognitive psychologist Steve Pinker, a Freud critic, speaks for many of us when he writes that "the idea that boys want to sleep with their mothers strikes most men as the silliest thing they have ever heard."[23] Contemporary scholarly assessments of the Freudian system can be harsh, as this one in a 1996 issue of *Psychological Science*: "There is literally nothing to be said, scientifically or therapeutically, to the advantage of the entire Freudian system or any of its component dogmas."[24]

Despite the relative obsolescence of many Freudian particulars, Freud's more general influence on contemporary culture remains profound. Freud critic John Kihlstrom asserts that "more than Einstein or Watson and Crick, more than Hitler or Lenin, Roosevelt or Kennedy, more than Picasso, Eliot, or Stravinsky, more than the Beatles or Bob Dylan, Freud's influence on modern culture has been profound and long-lasting."[25] If Freud was so wrong in his details and methods, then how could he continue to exert so powerful an influence on society?

Perhaps most importantly, Freud popularized the idea of the unconscious or subconscious mind as more significant in determining actions than the conscious will or mind. Freud was not the first person to develop an understanding of the unconscious, but his work transformed the way we understand the causes of human behavior. Although subsequent work in psychology (such as B. F. Skinner on the importance of environmental stimuli) has pointed to other influences, Freud's insights on the unconscious remain profoundly central.

Relatedly, Freud left a lasting mark on the study of human psychology by stressing that the brain or mind is not a single, unified organ or control unit but consists of different parts that often vie with each other. Although Freud's classification into ego, id, and superego has lost currency, the underlying observation about multiple, competing sources of thought or will in the same mind is essential to modern psychology. (As it was to the apostle Paul, who explained in Romans 7 that multiple wills contended within him.)

At a popular cultural level, Freudian concepts about the unconscious have infiltrated popular usage to the point of transforming everyday speech. When people allude to "Freudian slips," "Oedipus complex," "cathartic releases," "death wishes," "phallic symbols," "anal retentiveness," and "defense mechanisms," they pay homage to Freud and accept his theories as descriptive of psychological reality. Pundits regularly indulge Freud's theories, especially as to public figures they dislike. When President Trump famously tweeted the gibberish word *covfefe*, an obvious typographical error, the social media lit up with speculation about what this "Freudian slip" revealed about Trump's subconscious. This followed on years of pundits speculating about what President Obama's jokes reveal about his hidden thoughts, or how George W. Bush's relationship with his father shaped his presidency. In 2012, *New York Times* columnist Maureen Dowd asserted in an op-ed titled "Oedipus Rex Complex" that "American politics bristles with oedipal drama"[26] and then eased a suite of contemporary political figures onto the couch for a little lay psychoanalysis. Fun stuff!

The fact that Freudian theories are so ribald has surely contributed to their cultural longevity. It's often hard to tell whether people are asserting Freudian theories sincerely or satirically. (A personal anecdote: When I was a rookie law professor, I was invited to debate another lawyer on a legal and economic topic. Halfway through the debate, my opponent swerved from the debate topic and delivered a Freudian analysis of me to the smirking and snickering audience of two hundred. It seems more amusing to me now than it did then!)

That many of Freud's theories have proven scientifically and medically unreliable has done little to dent their acceptance as cultural memes. Nor has the obsolescence of many of Freud's psychological theories, on which his theory of religion was predicated, dented the veneration with which many skeptics and atheists hold *The Future of an Illusion.* As we saw in chapter 4 on Darwin, atheist Richard Dawkins titled his best-selling assault on religious belief *The God Delusion*, arguing that belief in God was not only ignorant but a kind of pervasive sickness in need of a cure. Sound familiar?

So what is the contemporary Christian to do with Sigmund Freud? It seems time to move beyond the more shocking and offensive sexual aspects of theories, many of which no longer enjoy currency with psychologists. There was much more to Freud than the Oedipus complex, much of it even resonating deeply with the Bible's teaching. In the end, the Christian must view Freud's life and work as tragic. He was a brilliant man, abused on account of his race, who suffered a great deal of physical and mental pain in his sad lifetime. Certainly, Freud meant to be no friend to the church, and many Christian criticisms of the man and his ideas are well warranted. But that does not have to stop us from absorbing his work and using even his erroneous arguments to sharpen our unfolding search for God's truth. As Pfister once wrote to Freud, "A powerful-minded opponent of religion is certainly of more service to it than a thousand useless supporters" (38). Or as Joseph said to his brothers, "What you meant for evil, God meant for good" (Gen. 50:20). Many of Freud's views may have been erroneous, and some offensive to Christians, but there is much in his work that should interest rather than repel the church.

CHAPTER 7

Joseph Campbell's *Hero with a Thousand Faces*: Christianity As an (Almost) Enlightened Myth

"The old-time religion belongs to another age, another people, another set of human values, another universe. By going back you throw yourself out of sync with history."

Joseph Campbell
The Power of Myth (1987)

Two men huddled under television lights in a den at filmmaker George Lucas's Skywalker Ranch. The year was 1987, and their intellectual engagement at the spiritual home of the *Star Wars* movies dazzled with all the glamour that Hollywood could muster. Not only was their dialogue physically set to evoke the ethos of the world's most popular film series, but the resulting book was championed at the Doubleday publishing house by Jacqueline Kennedy Onassis, the widow of President John F. Kennedy and the closest thing to American royalty at that time or since. Eventually, millions of people would view the taped interviews on PBS and millions more would read the book transcription of their dialogue.

The two conversants were veteran journalist Bill Moyers and Joseph Campbell, a retired professor of comparative religion at Sarah Lawrence College and perhaps the world's leading expert on the myths of different civilizations. Over the course of the lengthy interview, Campbell meandered through the world of mythology, weaving together a tapestry of common meaning from the stories of disparate cultures spread over time and space. Moyers, seminary trained and a former Baptist minister, conducted the interviews with an air of earnest puzzlement, like a child struggling to make sense of profound mysteries at the fringes of his ken.

Periodically, the conversation turned to Christianity—the stuff that Moyers had preached years before from the pulpit in Weir, Texas. Playing the foil to Campbell's emphatic denunciation of "old-time" and literal views of religion, Moyers purported to push back whenever Campbell strayed too far in unsettling longstanding theological traditions. At one juncture, Campbell explained that Jesus' ascension into heaven should be understood as just the opposite of the Savior rising upwards toward ethereal realms in the firmament. Campbell explained that was impossible, since we know from physics that there is no such place above us:

> But if you read "Jesus ascended to heaven" in terms of its metaphoric connotation, you see that he has gone inward—not into outer space but into inward space, to the place from which all being comes, into the consciousness that is the source of all things, the kingdom of heaven within. The images are outward, but their reflection is inward. The point is that we should ascend with him by going inward.

Moyers voiced the obvious objection of orthodox Christianity:

> Aren't you undermining one of the great traditional doctrines of the classic Christian faith—that the burial and the resurrection of Jesus prefigures our own?

Campbell had him right where he wanted him. With a tone somewhere between exuberant and irritated, he snapped back:

> That would be a mistake in the reading of the symbol. That is reading the words in terms of prose instead of in terms of poetry, reading the metaphor in terms of the denotation instead of the connotation.[1]

By the end of the PBS series, Campbell had given millions of Christians in his audience exactly what they "needed" to escape from the strict rigidity of "old-time religion" while still thinking of themselves as Christian. Christianity could still be "true" so long as it was understood metaphorically along with all of the other great world myths. After all, there was nothing really unique in Christianity any more than in other religion. All religions, all mythological systems, all folktales, rituals, and mystical practices were part of one overarching "Monomyth" that expressed the conscious and subconscious mind of the human race. Freed from the chains of orthodox Christianity—from its fundamentalist rigidity, doctrinal cruelty, unbending dogmas, and archaic morality—enlightened Christians were liberated to live by Joseph Campbell's mantra: to "follow your bliss."

Joseph Campbell's message resonates today with the children of postmodernism, including millions who never read his books or saw his PBS show, but who absorbed his message through the osmosis of Hollywood and popular culture. For those pining for unattached spirituality, Campbell's message offers the perfect panacea—a sense that there is deep meaning in the universe and perhaps even in the Christian religion, but that it is free from the fetters and strictures of conventional religion. Of all of the books studied here, Campbell's may pose the greatest threat to the church, because it offers a message that guts orthodox Christian belief while going down as sweetly as honey.

FROM BUFFALO BILL TO POSTMODERN GURU

The man who became America's leading postmodernist spiritual guru had a surprisingly conventional start. Joseph Campbell was born in White Plains, New York, in 1904 and raised in a middle-class Irish Catholic family. Campbell spent his high school years at the Canterbury School, a Catholic residential school in Connecticut, where he received a traditional Catholic education. His Catholic rearing, particularly the rich symbolic pageantry of Catholic Christian thought, would stamp a deep impression on him.

But young Joseph quickly found that his strongest attraction was not to the conventional symbolism of Christianity but to the wilder, fiercer symbolism of Old America. At the age of seven, Joseph went to a Buffalo Bill's Wild West Show. As Campbell would later write, although the cowboys were supposed to be the stars of the show, his life became transformed by a different element in the show—the Native Americans: "I became fascinated, seized, obsessed, by the figure of a naked American Indian with his ear to the ground, a bow and arrow in his hand, and a look of special knowledge in his eyes."[2] So was launched a lifelong love affair with the rituals, myths, and traditions of first the Native American peoples and then of the people of the world. By the age of ten, Campbell had read every book on American Indians in the children's section of his local library and the entire multivolume *Reports of the Bureau of American Ethnology*. As a child, he would wander the vast halls of the American Museum of Natural History in Manhattan, fascinated with totem poles and Indian masks.

In college at Columbia, Campbell turned toward a yet older world, focusing on medieval literature (when he wasn't playing in a jazz band and becoming a star runner). After obtaining a master's degree in Arthurian literature from Columbia, Campbell traveled to Europe on fellowships, spending time in Paris and Munich. It was late in the Roaring Twenties, on the verge of the Great Depression, and Europe exposed Campbell to modernist influences in art, literature, and psychology—such as Pablo Picasso, James Joyce, Thomas Mann, Sigmund Freud, and Carl Jung—that would profoundly shape his view of the world. According to the Joseph Campbell Foundation:

> These encounters would eventually lead him to theorize that all myths are the creative products of the human psyche, that artists are a culture's mythmakers, and that mythologies are creative manifestations of humankind's universal need to explain psychological, social, cosmological, and spiritual realities.[3]

His return to the United States coincided with the start of the Great Depression in 1929, a fact with considerable providential significance in Campbell's intellectual development. Unable to find steady work as a teacher, Campbell spent the larger part of the next five years aimlessly traveling the country, playing in a saxophone band, spending time along the way in the company of the novelist John Steinbeck, or cloistered away in a rustic cottage reading and writing. Interestingly for a man who went on to become the most influential expert on comparative mythology in recent memory, Campbell never earned a PhD. As Moyers would later recall, Campbell "gave up on the pursuit of a doctorate and went instead into the woods to read" (*PM* xv).

It was not until 1934 that Campbell finally found steady employment, but when he did it was for life. Sarah Lawrence College, then a women's college in Westchester County, New York, offered Campbell a teaching position in the literature department—a post he would hold until his retirement thirty-eight years later. Over his career as a scholar, Campbell collaborated on a large body of work in world mythology: participating in the creation of books on a wide array of topics, from religious thought in India, to Native American folklore, to a commentary on *Grimm's Fairy Tales*. Campbell also served as general editor of the papers of Heinrich Zimmer, an influential scholar of the art, religion, and philosophy of India. Campbell soured somewhat on Hinduism after visiting India in 1954 and observing its abject poverty, but he remained enamored of Buddhism to his death.

The book that put Campbell on the map was the first one he wrote on his own: *The Hero with a Thousand Faces*, first published in 1949. Borrowing a phrase from James Joyce, Campbell posited that that all heroic myths share a universal pattern—a Monomyth. All heroes, from Odysseus to Jesus, set out on the same archetypal hero's journey, passing through the same stages in the cosmic mythic cycle. According to Campbell, the Monomyth relates not only the metaphorical story of individual heroes but entire cultures as well. Thus it reveals the subconscious pattern of all human striving for meaning, whether individual or collective. It was, in short, an astonishingly broad unifying theory of human religion and mythology across time and space.

Over the second half of the twentieth century, *Hero* gradually snowballed in influence and reputation, even as Campbell moved onto other topics in comparative mythology. Eventually, the book would be translated into over twenty languages and sell over a million copies worldwide. As we will see shortly, however, although brilliantly written and full of fascinating stories, *Hero* is an academic book, one that takes scholarly convention seriously and does not aim for popular accessibility. The broad popularization of the ideas presented in *Hero* became possible only with the Bill Moyers PBS series, *The Power of Myth*, and the accompanying book by the same name.

Moyers and Campbell met in the late 1970s when Moyers was taping a television show at the Museum of Natural History and was struck by Campbell's power as a storyteller and teacher. He vowed to pursue Campbell for a full set of interviews based on *The Hero with a Thousand Faces*. The interviews finally materialized eight years later. George Lucas and Campbell had become good friends after Lucas, acknowledging the great debt he owed Campbell for the *Star*

Wars mythology, invited Campbell to a screening of the trilogy. The *Power of Myth* interviews were taped in 1985 and 1986, primarily at the Skywalker Ranch, but also at the Museum of Natural History where Campbell's mythic consciousness had been so shaped as a boy. Much material had to be cut to create the six-hour series; Campbell was such a sublime raconteur of myths and stories that the interviews might have gone on for days and days.

Campbell did not live to see the release of *The Power of Myth* program or book. He died of esophageal cancer in 1987 at his retirement home in Honolulu, Hawaii, aged eighty-three (in the company of his wife of forty-nine years, the accomplished dance choreographer Jean Erdman). Although the couple had no children, Campbell left behind a vast array of intellectual disciples (more on this to come). His memorial service, held—where else—at the Museum of Natural History, included a percussion performance by Mickey Hart, the drummer for the rock-and-roll band the Grateful Dead and a reading of poetry, accompanied by dulcimer, by the poet Robert Bly.

Alas, an incident following Campbell's death cast shadows on his tremendous reputation and legacy. In a September 1989 essay in the *New York Review of Books*, a writer for *The New Yorker*, Brendan Gill, accused Campbell of anti-Semitism, racism, social conservatism, and espousing banal selfishness. Bill Moyers angrily leapt to the deceased Campbell's defense, and exonerating commentary poured in from Campbell's former students, colleagues, and acquaintances. Still, a few voices supported Gill's recollection by reciting various comments by Campbell, such as during the time of the first lunar landing that "the moon would be a good place to put the Jews."[4] As with many such matters, the ultimate record is inconclusive on Campbell's overall character, although enough specific testimony has emerged to bolster some of Gill's claims. Ironically, given the ostensible "progressivism" of his religious views, Campbell's social and political views seem to have been staunchly conservative and at times included elements of racism.

But if it were ours to judge *the man*—and it is not (Matt.7:1)—perhaps we should judge Campbell by his best deeds rather than his worst. And in his best work—undoubtedly *The Hero with a Thousand Faces*—there is no shortage of important *things* for the Christian to judge (1 Cor. 2:15).

THE MONOMYTH AND ITS LIMITATIONS

The Hero with a Thousand Faces represents Campbell's effort to unify all of the religions, mythologies, legends, and folk stories of the world into what he called "Mankind's one great story." Campbell was well aware that his effort to unify so many disparate systems of thought into one overarching narrative would meet resistance, both from scholars who would accuse him of banal reductionism and, more ferociously, from religious adherents who would accuse him of pillaging and then destroying their unique claims to truth. But Campbell relished a good clash and ran headlong into these challenges.

Tellingly, Campbell began the preface to the 1949 edition with a quotation from Freud to the effect that "the truths contained in religious doctrines are after all so distorted and systematically disguised."[5] To emphasize at the outset Freud's claim about *the truth* in religion set Campbell's book on a very different course from the one we saw Freud charting in the last chapter: characterizing belief in God as an illusion. Unlike Freud, Campbell's approach to myth and religion would be positive and supportive. "As we are told in the Vedas (holy books of Hinduism)," wrote Campbell, "Truth is one, the sages speak of it by many names" (*HTF* xiii). It was true—all of it! But it had to be true in a subtler way than most people recognized, hence the nod to Freud's view about distorted lenses.

Hero's prologue grounded Campbell's claim of universality in Freud's and Jung's work on the human subconscious. Why is it, Campbell asked, that we hear "one shape-shifting but marvelously constant story" whether we're listening to a "red-eyed witch doctor of the Congo," "sonnets of the mystic Lao-tse," a "bizarre Eskimo fairy tale," or an argument by Thomas Aquinas? The answer, Campbell asserted, lies in the fact that the elements and symbols of religion and mythology "are not manufactured"; they are not arbitrary, inventive, or creative acts of individuals or cultures. Rather, "they are spontaneous productions of the psyche," welling up from the same subconscious patterns that indwell every human brain (*HTF* 1). Campbell thus provided a nominally scientific account for the universality of human mythic and religious themes: they all originated from the same subconscious pool.

At the center of Campbell's account stood the hero. For Campbell, heroes are not merely protagonists who give stories their personal motivation. A hero is a hero—or, rather, he becomes a hero—when he performs universal archetypes and hence "battles past his personal and local historical limitations to the generally valid," thus expressing the universal human story. Campbell asserted that, across all human mythology, heroes follow a common path of the Monomyth. Broadly speaking, the hero's journey consists of three stages—separation, initiation, and return. Each stage includes five or six sub-stages. The separation stage includes a call to adventure, the hero's initial refusal of the call, supernatural aid, the crossing of the first threshold, and the belly of the whale, in which the hero descends into the "realm of night." The initiation stage includes the road of trials, the meeting with the goddess, woman as temptress, atonement with the Father, apotheosis, and the ultimate boon. Finally, the return and reintegration phase includes refusal to return or denial of the world, the magic flight, rescue from without, the crossing of the return threshold, the master of the two worlds, and the freedom to live.

Campbell spends the bulk of *Hero* attempting to demonstrate that these stages and sub-stages are universally represented in mythology and religion: "Whether the hero be ridiculous or sublime, Greek or barbarian, gentile or Jew, his journey varies little in essential plan" (*HTF* 30). If an element was not explicitly stated in a hero story, then "it is bound to be somehow or other implied," or so claims Campbell (*HTF* 30). But, frustratingly for the skeptic of Campbell's account, the book's narrative structure makes it challenging to test Campbell's claim that all hero stories follow the same archetype to a T. The book proceeds sub-stage by sub-stage and musters multiple examples from disparate myths to illustrate each sub-stage. By the book's end, the reader has certainly encountered a rich and fascinating set of mythical stories, and a fair amount of evidence for the presence of archetypal elements in different myths. But rarely, if ever, does the book take a particular hero story from beginning to end and demonstrate its compliance with all seventeen sub-stages, which makes it hard either to credit or discredit Campbell's claim that all hero stories faithfully follow the same pattern.

For instance, readers of this book might be particularly interested to learn whether the biblical account of Jesus performs Campbell's

archetypal canon, proceeding systematically through the three main
stages and seventeen sub-stages. Campbell repeatedly assures us that
it does, and Jesus figures prominently, even opportunistically, in *Hero*.
He appears prominently when the archetypes seem to suit, as with
respect to rescue from without (the Resurrection), master of the two
worlds (the Transfiguration), and atonement with the Father (the
Eucharist). But one might feel entitled to demand evidence of Jesus'
initial refusal of the call, his meeting with the goddess, and encounter
with woman as temptress (are substitutions permitted in the form
of the decidedly masculine Satan in the wilderness?), among other
things. *Hero* provides no such evidence.

One can therefore question whether Campbell met the burden
he established for himself. It would not be enough for Campbell to
prove common patterns or archetypes among world myths or religions,
which wouldn't be a particularly novel or surprising claim. Since Campbell sought to show that all myths and religions are part of one great
story plucked from the universal human subconscious, he needed to
establish the structural uniformity of all myths and religions. To use an
analogy, suppose a geneticist were seeking to establish that a group of
people were descended from the same region. It wouldn't do to point
out that they had had many genes in common, since all people have
many genes in common. He would need to establish a degree of consistent uniformity in their genes and that this pattern was not shared
by others. As we shall see, subsequent critics have complained that
Campbell failed to meet the high burden he assigned himself.

IS JESUS' STORY PART OF THE MONOMYTH?

Campbell's account of the Monomyth challenges orthodox Christian thinking in two ways, (one specific and the other general) At the
specific level, Campbell directly challenged the traditional Christian
account of Jesus as a unique historical figure whose life and death
lay at the fulcrum of human history. According to Campbell, Jesus is
" 'the king's son' who has come to know who he is and therewith has
entered into the exercise of his proper power—'God's son,' who has
learned to know how much that title means" (*HTF* 31). But though
Campbell had no trouble in referring to Jesus as divine, that was

because Jesus' divinity, per Campbell, was symbolic of humanity's common divinity. Jesus, as the archetypal hero, is "symbolical of that divine creative and redemptive image which is hidden within us all" (*HTF* 31). Campbell allows for two interpretations of Jesus' story—that he was "a man who by dint of austerities and meditation obtained wisdom," or "a god [who] descended and took upon himself the enactment of a human career" so that we could realize our "own immanent divinity" (HTF 275). But Campbell's interpretation left no room for a historical Jesus, the Son of God, born to redeem humanity from sin through his death and resurrection and his ascension into heaven to rule with God the Father forever. Speaking explicitly of orthodox Christianity, Campbell wrote that "whenever the poetry of myth is interpreted as biography, history, or science, it is killed. . . . Such a blight has certainly descended on the Bible and on a great part of the Christian cult" (*HTF* 213). At the casuistic level then, Campbell pitted his account of the Monomyth against orthodox Christianity, or what he pejoratively derided as "the old-time religion."

Campbell's anti-orthodox interpretation of his Monomyth hypothesis can be rebutted on interpretive grounds: What gives Campbell the authority to insist that the Christian story cannot be understood literally or historically just because other world stories share the same patterns or archetypes as the Christian story? It is not at all uncommon for historically documented biographies to share archetypal patterns with mythical stories. Claims of ahistoricity based on a narrative's conformity to an archetypal pattern are often demonstrably overstated. For example, the amateur anthropologist Lord Raglan developed a list of twenty-two common traits ostensibly shared by heroes across cultures, myths, and religions. He claimed that the higher a figure's score, the more likely the figure was mythical.[6] But the folklorist Francis Utley demonstrated that Abraham Lincoln fit all twenty-two of Raglan's traits, which would suggest that Lincoln was a mythical figure.[7] Myths are most powerful when they resonate with lived experiences, so we should not expect myths and true history to diverge excessively.

There is a more general sense in which *Hero* challenges orthodox Christian thinking. Whatever Campbell's personal interpretation of his Monomyth hypothesis for Christianity, there remains the possibility that the sheer volume of mythological and folkloric data collected in *Hero* reveals the Christian story to have been copied from earlier stories—that it is a fourth, fifth, sixth, or thousandth edition of a story that has been told since the earliest human campfires and that will be told, in contextually adapted repetition, until a supernova or comet snuffs out the human race. In other words, if Campbell's work demonstrates that the Christian account of Jesus was largely copied from earlier mythical stories, wouldn't that suggest that the Christian account was metaphorical rather than historical, that it was a borrowed and repackaged story rather than an original account of things that actually happened? Many scholars of religion have leveled such accusations against Christianity in recent years.

Maybe, but couldn't the opposite lesson equally be drawn from the universality of themes in the Christian story—that any authentically divine plan of redemption for the human race would correspond to known tropes and archetypes, that mythical stories would foreshadow the true story because the mythical stories and true stories addressed the same human needs, desires, and longings? Scripture itself is no obstacle to such an interpretation. Far from claiming idiosyncratic or mystical truths, the Scriptures themselves claim universal accessibility to the core facts about God and his work in the world through observation of nature and the exercise of right reason. For example, in Romans 1, the apostle Paul describes God's invisible qualities, essential power, and divine nature as being knowable from observation of the physical world so that people are without excuse for rejecting God, even absent special revelation. Christian writers, such as the medieval theologian Saint Thomas Aquinas, derived from such passages the existence of a natural moral law accessible to all people. Similarly, C. S. Lewis argued in *Mere Christianity* that homogeneity in moral attitudes across cultures and times supports the Christian claim to an objective, God-given conscience. From a scriptural perspective, it would therefore not be surprising to learn that many cultures tell stories about atonement with a father figure through the shedding of blood, for example, since the need for such atonement is discernable from study of God's creation, conscience, and the exercise of right reason.

In this regard, it is important to distinguish between Campbell's assertion of certain *facts*—namely, that all world myths march in lockstep through a common set of archetypes—and his *interpretation* of this alleged uniformity. That virgin birth stories are common to most or all world mythologies is a claimed fact; it is subject to examination through critical evidence and falsification or validation. That the ostensible ubiquity of virgin birth stories means that the account of Jesus' birth must be taken metaphorically and not literally is not a fact; it is a subjective interpretation of the facts. Orthodox Christians can surely agree that Campbell's interpretation of the facts is wrong, and indeed spiritually and morally dangerous. But it is less clear whether orthodox Christians must also find threatening his underlying factual claim of archetypal homogeneity in the world's mythologies. Reasonable Christians might feel threatened on the grounds that the Christian story's authenticity rests on its status as original, unique, and unparalleled in human history. But reasonable Christians might also take the contrary view—that the Greatest Story Ever Told embodies and fulfills the fears, hopes, and aspirations of every other human story and that its consonance with them tends to prove its authenticity rather than call it into doubt.

A brief thought experiment may help put this matter into perspective. Imagine that you were preparing for a debate with an atheist in which your job was to defend the claims of orthodox Christianity to a "neutral" audience. Your debate coach hands you a file labeled "evidence from world mythology." In it, you find information supporting one of two opposite claims: (1) that the key features of the Christian story are unique and unparalleled in world mythology; or (2) that many patterns in the Christian story resonate strongly with pervasive archetypes in world mythology. Which version would you rather find in the file? Which one would better help you make your case for the authenticity of Christianity?

As a lawyer who is frequently involved in debates and formal arguments, I am still unsure which version of the file would be strategically more useful. A deft debater might make effective use of either. Of course, the Christian mission is to redeem the world for Christ, not just to win debates. But this thought experiment hopefully shows that the core of Campbell's factual claim in *Hero*—of archetypal homogeneity among world myths, including Christianity—need not be taken as necessarily antithetical to the Christian message. Under one construction, the homogeneity hypothesis actually supports the gospel's authenticity.

This was certainly the view of two of the greatest Christian mythologists—C. S. Lewis and J. R. R. Tolkien. Lewis and Tolkien both argued that Christianity should be understood as the one true myth in a broad, ancient mythological tradition. As Lewis put it, "The heart of Christianity is a myth which is also a fact."[8] In *Till We Have Faces*, Lewis's last and arguably greatest novel, Lewis retold the Greek myth of Cupid and Psyche through a Christian lens, breathing Christian meaning into a pagan story. Tolkien, a devout Catholic, argued that myths or "fairy stories" presented truth within fiction by showcasing internally consistent actions within magical parameters.[9] For Tolkien and Lewis, then, the ubiquity of mythological themes and patterns across time and place should be no embarrassment to the church, but rather confirmation that the true gospel message resonates with thousands of other stories grasping at the truth through a glass darkly.

A "New Age Cult"?

Did Joseph Campbell rock the church? By the second half of the twentieth century, the American church had become so denominationally, theologically, ideologically, politically, and culturally fractured that one would have to first define "church" to answer that question. Certainly, large swaths of the broadly Christian community, including self-identified Protestants and Catholics and (again broadly) Christian scholars of religion, found Campbell's message enlivening and worthy of serious study and contemplation. Several academic volumes sympathetically contemplated the relevance of Campbell's teaching for contemporary Christian thought.[10]

For example, Brian McDermott, a Catholic clergyman, systematic theologian, and theology professor, asked whether a "reflective Christian" who was both attracted to Campbell's worldview but concerned about its implications for the uniqueness of Jesus could reconcile these ostensibly opposing viewpoints.[11] While criticizing Campbell for being so enamored of "unity and universality" that he failed "to do justice to diversity,"[12] McDermott nonetheless argued that the core of Campbell's teaching could be accepted by Catholic Christians in the "inclusive" spirit of the Second Vatican Council, which allowed for the assertion that "Jesus Christ is the unsurpassable revelation of God but that salvation from God is offered to all people regardless of their location in history or their explicit beliefs, provided that they are true to the impulses of divine grace at work in their conscience."[13]

In contrast to such sympathetic treatment from some Christian corners, conservative Christians saw in Campbell's message a grave spiritual and cultural threat. Mortimer Adler, an eminent American philosopher who was ethnically Jewish and a convert to Christianity, sounded a typical tone when he scathingly took Campbell to task in a 1992 article in *National Review*. Mortimer asserted that Campbell's "understanding of the Christian creed and theology was puerile. In that field he was an ignoramus."[14] Moreover, Campbell's claim that all religions were factually and logically false—and only true in a metaphorical sense—was supported not by scientific or logical argumentation, but rather by "purely rhetorical means, ill-concealed innuendo intended to discredit, not disprove, religious beliefs." Finally, Adler argued that Campbell's famous maxim to "follow your bliss" was an invitation to "do whatever you want to do if it gives you pleasure" and represented "the lowest debasement of twentieth-century culture."

In evangelical Protestant circles, the mainstream view holds that Campbell represents the leading edge of a "New Age" assault on Christian truth. Typical are the comments of Elliot Miller of the Christian Research Institute, who dismissed the *Power of Myth* PBS series as a "bold venture into New Age propagandizing" with "heavy 'doses' of New Age indoctrination."[15] Similarly, writing in *Christianity Today*, Douglas Groothius, a leading evangelical critic of New Age ideology, described Campbell as a "prophet of the New Age."[16] To the extent that students at Christian liberal arts or Bible colleges have encountered Joseph Campbell, it is likely to have been as part of a warning against New Ageism or the creeping influence of Eastern philosophy on Western and Christian thought.[17]

The most comprehensive Christian rebuttal to Campbell, *Myth Conceptions: Joseph Campbell and the New Age*, was published in 1995 by social critic Tom Snyder.[18] Snyder acknowledged Campbell's vast contemporary influence, noting that he may "have had more influence on American religious thought than any other contemporary writer" and that his writings have become "handbooks of spirituality to New Agers, neo-pagans, environmentalists, intellectuals, and nominal Jews and Christians."[19] Snyder rebutted Campbell on a succession of grounds. First, he argued that Campbell's arguments were internally contradictory. Campbell argued that anyone claiming to have found absolute truth was necessarily wrong, but Campbell's own assertion was assertion of absolute truth (i.e., "It is absolutely true that anyone claiming to have found absolute truth is wrong"). Second, Snyder argued that Campbell had misinterpreted the meaning of transcendence and myth, claiming them to be inherently non-rational and contradictory experiences when, claimed Snyder, many cultures recognize a rational component to transcendent experience and mythical storytelling. Third, Snyder showed that although Campbell claimed (and Moyers claimed for Campbell) to be entirely non-ideological and nontheological, Campbell dogmatically embraced an anti-orthodox ideology and a pantheistic theology. Thus "Campbell hypocritically condemns other people for being dogmatic and narrow-minded about truth, God, religion, and morality, but he himself is guilty of doing the same thing."[20] Finally, Snyder argued that Campbell's ideological and theological commitments led him into consequential errors: He completely misinterpreted and distorted Christian teaching and practice, and espoused a morally bankrupt moral relativism with potentially devastating social consequences.

Graciously, Snyder conceded that "not everything Campbell wrote or said was wrong."[21] He allowed that Campbell had actually said some "profound things about the human condition and the role of heroes throughout human history."[22] Bill Moyers (the former Baptist minister) went even further, insisting that Campbell had actually strengthened his Christian faith. In *Power of Myth*, Moyers told Campbell: "Far from undermining my faith your work in mythology has liberated my faith from the cultural prisons to which it is sentenced" (*PM* 55).

If Campbell had indeed strengthened Moyers's Christian faith, it is hard to believe he did so intentionally. One need not stretch to find an anti-Christian message in Campbell's interpretation of the Monomyth; one can take it straight from Campbell himself. Campbell's authorized biographers quote him as saying, "Clearly, Christianity is opposed fundamentally and intrinsically to everything that I am working and living for. Krishna is a much better teacher and model than Christ."[23] From the abundance of the heart, the mouth speaketh. However scholars or prophets of popular culture might wrap Campbell's message as benign and inclusive of all religions, there is little

doubt that Campbell himself viewed orthodox Christians—the pur-
veyors of "the old-time religion"—as the enemy.

HERO IN THE LIMELIGHT

Joseph Campbell's work has had a mixed reception among academic experts on comparative religion, myth, literature, and folklore.
Many intellectual voices credit Campbell's Monomyth hypothesis as
a serious scholarly endeavor that offers a plausible unifying theory
of world mythology. He has been called the Western world's "foremost authority" on mythology[24] and a "sage" who brought mythology to popular culture in the same way that Carl Sagan popularized
science.[25]

Others take Campbell to task for gross overgeneralizations, such
as failure to distinguish between myths, legends, and folklore and
overclaiming the universality of mythic archetypes. Among the leading critical voices was the distinguished folklorist Alan Dundes, a
professor at the University of California Berkeley. In 2004, the year
before his death, Dundes gave a keynote address at the American
Folklore Society in which he pilloried Campbell's central claim in
Hero—that there is such a thing as a universal Monomyth that binds
all human stories over time.[26] According to Dundes, "There is not
one single myth that is universal." Dundes faults Campbell for "playing fast and loose" with stories, conveniently omitting angles that
don't fit his narrative, and blatantly misrepresenting stories in order
to make them fit. For example, Dundes argues that there is no universal virgin birth archetype and that Campbell's assertion to the contrary is pure "wishful thinking." There are no such stories from Africa,
Siberia, Polynesia, Melanesia, aboriginal Australia, or New Guinea,
even though those regions abound with myths. Indeed, the one example Campbell gives of a virgin birth account originating in Africa
is a story "that tells of the first man having intercourse with his wives
and daughters to produce children and animals, hardly a convincing
example of a virgin birth." (The distinguished Princeton University
New Testament scholar J. Gresham Machen made the same point in
1930 in his *The Virgin Birth of Christ*—none of the pagans stories often
cited as virgin birth instances are, in fact, virgin birth stories.)

Such academic criticism, however, has not dented the enthusiastic reception for Campbell's ideas in popular culture. Indeed, it is hard to overstate the influence of Campbell's work on Hollywood and pop culture more generally. Christopher Volger, an influential Hollywood development executive, has suggested that *Hero* may turn out to be the most influential book of the twentieth century—a claim that is surely debatable as an intellectual matter, but not far from the truth when it comes to Hollywood.

Nowhere in popular culture has Campbell's influence been more pronounced than in the *Star Wars* movies. George Lucas had already written two drafts of the *Star Wars* screenplay when he rediscovered *The Hero's Journey*, which he had read years before in college. Reading it anew gave him the impetus to organize what would become the *Star Wars* brand into a single, cohesive mythology. With a little creative stretching, the original *Star Wars* movie checks all of the boxes in Campbell's Departure-Initiation-Return paradigm for our hero Luke Skywalker. For example: Call to adventure (Luke discovers Princess Leia's hologram message); refusal of call (Luke has excuses that make him sound like his uncle); supernatural aid (Obi-Wan rescues Luke from the Sand People and trains him in the way of the Force); crossing the first threshold (Luke leaves his home planet of Tatooine); belly of the whale (Luke almost dies in the unforgettable trash compactor on the first Death Star); and so forth. A version of *Hero* published in 1977, the year the first *Star Wars* movie was released, portrayed actor Mark Hamill as Luke Skywalker on the cover. Christian critics of *Star Wars*' religious message have seen in the movies clear evidence of Campbell's pantheistic and moral relativist handiwork.[27] In the series' most recent episode—*The Last Jedi*—the venerable Yoda casually burns a set of ancient Jedi religious texts, explaining that the old books held some wisdom but nothing indispensable. Campbell would doubtlessly have approved this adieu to the old-time religion. He created the theory; Lucas (and his successors) spread it to the masses through the big screen.

Campbell's influence on popular culture, however, has spread far beyond the *Star Wars* movies. *Hero* was also reportedly influential in the thinking of filmmaker Stanley Kubrick (*2001: A Space Odyssey*), novelist Richard Adams (*Watership Down*), and rock-and-roll stars Bob Dylan (and Nobel Laureate!?) and Jim Morrison. The iconic, cultish rock band the Grateful Dead were so profoundly influenced by Campbell's work that they held a weekend seminar with Campbell titled "From Ritual to Rapture, from Dionysus to the Grateful Dead" on Halloween weekend in 1986. Many fans of the popular ABC TV show *Lost* reported observing *The Hero's Journey* in the paths of story's central characters—an influence explicitly acknowledged by the show's creators. Pop culture thought leaders from literature, to music, to video games, to film and television have explicitly or implicitly embraced Campbell's heroic Monomyth and incorporated it into the cultural memes and messages they transmit.

Most contemporary American Christians have not read *The Hero with a Thousand Faces* or even encountered the more popularly accessible version of Campbell's work by watching *The Power of Myth*. Nonetheless, one would have to be almost entirely sheltered from contemporary popular culture to avoid encountering a presentation of Campbell's perspective. As Bob and Gretchen Passantino of Answers in Action ministries put it, "Whether you have heard of Joseph Campbell by name or not, you have had his message of the myth of Christianity preached to you countless times in countless ways."[28]

Why was Joseph Campbell so successful in captivating popular culture? The power of myth is the power of storytelling, and there is no doubt that Campbell was a supremely good storyteller. Deeply immersed in mythological tradition over time and space, he grasped the essential patterns that make for enthralling hero narratives—calls to adventure, reluctance, quests to distant realms, defeats, sacrifices, apotheoses—and packaged them in a way that could be easily appropriated by leading contemporary storytellers. Along the way, he also stole the opportunity to interpret his art as an irrefutable indictment of orthodox Christianity. Much of popular culture joined Bill Moyers in swallowing the interpretation along with the story.

But it doesn't have to be that way. As we have seen, Campbell's interpretation need not follow from his story. Campbell interpreted his Monomyth as evidence that the Christian story is every story. But couldn't we just as well say that every story is the Christian story? In the past, God chose to speak through such varied and imperfect vessels as a donkey (Num. 22), a burning bush (Exod. 3), and even a medium's séance (1 Sam. 28). Surely, he could choose to speak through a Monomyth as well.

CHAPTER 8

Conclusion: The Next Seven Books

*"As good almost kill a man as kill a good book: who kills
a man kills a reasonable creature, God's image; but
he who destroys a good book kills reason itself."*

John Milton
Areopagitica (1644)

We have now examined seven books, spread over nearly two thousand years, which rocked the church. Each one did so in a somewhat different way, and the church responded differently in different circumstances. And yet some common, unfortunate patterns emerge from this survey.

When the church had the political power to suppress a book through force of law and the state, it did—as in the cases of Valentinus, Galileo, and Voltaire. For contemporary readers accustomed to First Amendment and freedom of speech values, it's easy to criticize outright censorship as ineffective and counterproductive, given that each of these suppressed books went on to become a landmark of forbidden fruit and read with gleeful fascination by the curious. One might argue that our sample is not representative of the success of censorship since it includes books that, by definition, eventually got out, and who knows what other condemned works still lie buried in the sands of Egypt or rotting in a dank cellar in Rome? Even so, the measure of censorship's legitimacy cannot simply be how successful it is at burying offending works. In Galileo's case, we can confidently assert today that his scientific views were right and the church's were wrong. And while we may disagree with Valentinus's theology and lament Voltaire's ribald mockery, it is difficult with hindsight to see how the church was better off suppressing their work than engaging it.

With the rise of the Enlightenment followed by political liberalism in Europe, legal suppression became less available, but the church continued to attack offending works through other means. Character assassination or *ad hominem* attack has long been a favorite tactic to discredit rival ideas. As we saw, the church honed this practice with respect to Valentinus and later doubled down in personal assaults on the characters of Darwin, Freud, and Marx, often with anti-Semitic overtones. As to Voltaire, the church went even further, attempting to leverage its power over burial rights to secure the philosophe's retraction. Mean-spirited, coercive *ad hominem* assaults tend to reveal the attacker as worse than the attacked, however, and yield precisely the opposite of the intended result.

Suppression and personal attack are counterproductive strategies, but a third strategy—practiced by the church with respect to most of the books studied in this volume—is yet far more deleterious to the church's mission in the world. This tactic is to assert that the challenged work is flatly inconsistent with Christian doctrine, such that if the book were right, then Christianity would have to be wrong. This argument proves far too much and sets up the church for the dangerous counterattack—observed especially with respect to Darwin—that once some of the challenged author's claims are proven right, Christianity has been proven wrong. We do not need to credit the claims of a Darwin, Marx, Freud, or Campbell to worry about the effects of insisting that everything they teach is categorically inconsistent with the Bible. Now, in order to persuade scientists of the reasonableness of Christianity, we have to out-debate them on the theory of natural selection. The same goes for economic historians on dialectic materialism, psychologists on psychoanalysis and illusion, and cultural anthropologists on the commonality of myths. By erecting a do-or-die showdown with troubling intellectual works, the church unduly complicates the presentation of the gospel. When entering serious and important intellectual debates, Christians should generally avoid staking the gospel on the outcome—as if we frail vessels had the authority to stake the gospel on the rise and fall of human knowledge.

Fortunately, not every story we encountered in this survey spelled doom and gloom for the church. Along the rocky path through which our stories wended, we encountered examples of Christians who engaged positively with threatening works, exhibiting a generosity of spirit, discerning where truth lay amid falsity, and correcting error firmly but gently. Leading examples include: Oskar Pfister, who challenged Freud's atheism while embracing his therapeutic methods; Asa Gray, who insisted that any process of Darwinian evolution had to be guided by a Creator; and various twentieth-century Christian thinkers who understood that Marx's heated call for revolution, however misguided, sprang from legitimate political and economic grievances that required a sincere, effective, and humane answer. As we have seen, Christians can read and discuss even heretical, offensive, or dangerous books with the assurance that all truth is God's truth, and that any truth found amid error is still truth worth knowing.

To be sure, there are books Christians shouldn't read and indeed should actively oppose. Salacious works, which speak to base instincts rather than the rational mind, do not deserve our respect or attention (James 1:21). Nor do libelous or gossipy works that debase the reputation of others or spread malice rather than reason (Prov. 11:13; 2 Cor. 12:20). The Christian is also admonished to avoid foolish controversies about divisive matters (Titus 3:9). Political diatribes, ideological screeds, and obtuse theological polemics are good candidates for exclusion from the Christian's library. Of course, Christian parents, pastors, teachers, and others working with young people or the spiritually or intellectually immature have a responsibility to introduce difficult material in age- and maturity-appropriate manners to avoid confusion, error, and offense (1 Cor. 8; Rom. 14). My own children will be holding company with Aslan for quite some time before meeting Dr. Pangloss.

Still, the church's response to threatening books could stand a comprehensive reconsideration. The seven studied here are just the tip of the iceberg—selections from a two-thousand-year history in which hundreds of books were suppressed or attacked by Christians zealous to defend the faith. The Roman Catholic Church's *Index Librorum Prohibitorum* has alone hosted hundreds of titles. Although the Index was formally abolished in 1966, in coming years there will doubtless be many new works in science, theology, philosophy, politics, psychology, history, economics, and social thought that throw down the gauntlet to orthodox Christianity. As Christianity transitions from the majority religion—at least nominally—to an often derided minority faith in much of the Western world, we can expect many new encounters with books that rock the church. How, then, should we prepare to meet the next seven books?

JOHN MILTON AND THE LESSONS OF HISTORY

It is commonplace to recite philosopher George Santayana's wisdom that those who do not learn history are destined to repeat it, but just what lessons of history should the church heed? To conclude our study, we will turn to some wisdom about dangerous books from one of the greatest Christian writers of all time—the Puritan poet and polemicist John Milton, author of the sublime epic poem *Paradise Lost*.

Milton lived a dangerous life in perilous times for writers with strong and controversial opinions. Closely aligned with the Puritan and Parliamentary cause during Oliver Cromwell's Commonwealth, Milton went so far as to write a book, *Eikonoklastes*, justifying the regicide of Charles I. Following the monarchic restoration of Charles II, although Milton's life became endangered and he was briefly imprisoned, he was ultimately one of the few leading Cromwellian Republicans spared. But it was religion rather than politics that handed Milton some of his biggest troubles. In 1644, at the height of the English Civil War, Milton found himself frustrated in his efforts to publish tracts arguing for the liberalization of divorce law (springing out of Milton's own souring marriage), a position on which he found few Christian allies on either side of the Civil War. Although friendly to the Parliament, Milton vehemently opposed the 1643 Ordinance for the Regulating of Printing, which required authors to obtain a license from the government before their work could be published. Milton's 1644 tract *Areopagitica* would become the most famous defense of freedom of speech in Western history and perhaps the world.

Areopagitica is named after the *Areopagitikos*, a speech of the fifth-century BC Athenian orator who aimed to restore the influence of the Areopagus, an ancient Athenian council that met on a rocky outcrop of the same name. The Areopagus also has special resonance for Christians. As recorded in Acts 17, it was here that the apostle Paul made his famous defense of Christianity before the upper echelon of the Greek *intelligentsia*. Milton appropriated the Areopagus, famous for its robust freedom of speech and Paul's mission to the Gentiles, as the organizing symbol of his provocative tract.

The immediate focus of Milton's argument was free speech of a particular kind: legal freedom from prior restraint by the government. Milton argued that, even if it was sometimes appropriate to punish authors for publishing evil books, it was always inappropriate to require authors to get permission before publishing. The legal principle Milton sought to establish became the underpinning of the American Constitution's First Amendment. Though arguing for a specific version of legal freedom of speech, however, Milton's *Areopagitica* made two broader points that can inform a Christian view of potentially dangerous books. Milton argued that we should listen carefully before condemning books, because arguments that at first seem wrong could turn out to be right. And he argued that Christians can profit from reading even deeply erroneous works.

LISTEN FIRST

To Milton, freedom from prior restraint was critical because it meant that controversial works would be published and available for public scrutiny before any censor could act against them. Works that authorities might reflexively suppress because they bucked popular mores, poked sacred cows, or threatened traditional ways of thinking would be exposed to a broad readership before the censors could condemn them as treasonous, seditious, blasphemous, libelous, or indecent. Once the book was widely available for readership, the merits of the argument could be studied and discussed. True and meritorious assertions of fact or theory could be received, retained in memory, and passed on in conversation or new works, even if the authorities subsequently decided to suppress the original work and punish the author.

Unlike some modern free-speech advocates who take literally the maxim that "sticks and stones may break my bones but words will never harm me," Milton recognized that words and ideas have deadly power and that false words and ideas can corrupt even the soul. It should be "of the greatest concernment in the church and commonwealth, to have a vigilant eye how books demean themselves as well as men," wrote Milton, "for books are not absolutely dead things, but do contain a potency of life in them to be as active as that soul was whose progeny they are."[1] False words "are as lively, and as vigorously productive, as those fabulous dragon's teeth; and being sown up and down, may chance to spring up armed men" (102). Milton might have added, with the apostle James, that the tongue (and the quill or keyboard) has the power to light the fires of hell (James 3:6).

But if dangerous books have the power to destroy, then it's equally true, wrote Milton, that good books have the power of life. "As good almost kill a man as kill a good book; who kills a man kills a reasonable creature, God's image; but he who destroys a good book, kills reason itself, kills the image of God, as it were in the eye" (102). Indeed, a good book, argued Milton, is in some ways more valuable than the individual author, since the author is doomed to return to the dust, whereas "a good book is the precious life-blood of a master spirit, embalmed and treasured up on purpose to a life beyond life" (102).

If books are both dangerous and life-giving, then how is the Christian to interact with them? According to Milton, it's impossible to avoid the evil influences of books without also throwing out the good influences, since "good and evil we know in the field of this world grow up together almost inseparably; and the knowledge of good is so involved and interwoven with the knowledge of evil, and in so many cunning resemblances hardly to be discerned" (111). Thus the Christian should listen carefully to all sorts of arguments with a discerning spirit and, following Paul's admonition in 1 Thessalonians 5:21, "prove all things, hold fast that which is good." Though such open-mindedness will expose the Christian to the danger of falsehood, Milton finds assurances in Titus 1:15 that "to the pure all things are pure," which means that "not only meats and drinks, but all kind of knowledge whether of good or evil; the knowledge cannot defile, nor consequently the books, if the will and conscience be not defiled" (109). The Christian liberty celebrated in the New Testament includes the freedom to study even works that may contain false and dangerous teachings, confident that a spirit of discernment will identify truth and error and keep the heart and soul blameless from exposure to the malignant.

How would the last two thousand years of church history have looked if the church had adopted Milton's spirit with respect to dangerous books? The church still would have rejected error and heresy, but it would have done so more graciously, and indeed more effectively. Rather than banning, attacking, belittling, suppressing, and threatening, it would have listened first, exhibited an open mind, studied carefully, and credited truth even when nestled in falsity. Looking forward to the next two thousand years, the church will have many more opportunities to exhibit these virtues. Yes, books are dangerous—all of them are, whether their message is ultimately right or wrong. The Christian is called to test the spirits, not to avoid them (1 John 4:1), and the only way to test a book is to read it.

THERE IS PROFIT EVEN IN ERROR

As we have just seen, Milton argued that Christians should listen and read before condemning, since otherwise they risk suppressing the true and useful along with the erroneous. But Milton went even further and made a provocative but powerful point: There is profit even in error. The Christian should read dangerous books not only because they may contain some important truth, but also because even the falsehood they contain may be instructive to the Christian's mind, heart, and character.

Milton grounded this argument in biblical precedent, particularly "the examples of Moses, Daniel and Paul who were skillful in all the learning of the Egyptians, Chaldeans and Greeks, which could not probably be without reading their books of all sorts" (108). Encountering and understanding error, argued Milton, allows the Christian to grow in moral, intellectual, and spiritual strength. "He that can apprehend and consider vice with all her baits and pleasures, and yet abstain, and yet distinguish, and yet prefer that which is truly better, he is the true wayfaring[2] Christian" (111). Indeed, the Bible itself often "relates blasphemy not nicely" (112), for example when it reports the arguments of secular philosophers such as the Epicureans. Why then, asked Milton, should the Christian avoid engaging with anti-Christian writings?

Milton's argument draws abundant support from the biblical record. Consider, for example, the account of Daniel, Hananiah, Mishael, and Azariah (renamed Shadrach, Meshach, and Abednego by their Babylonian captors; see Dan. 1). They were given instruction in the "language and literature" of the Babylonians and, upon examination by King Nebuchadnezzar were found ten times wiser and more knowledgeable than the king's court magicians and diviners. It's customary to think of this story as an example of faith and constancy amid adversity, but have you ever stopped to ponder the content of the "language and literature" of the Babylonians? The Akkadian literary corpus that the young Jewish captives would have had to master included a large dose of pagan mythology (such as the *Epic of Gilgamesh*), texts teaching omens, divination, incantations, and astrology, and a variety of bawdy tales of human interactions with men, gods, beasts, and monsters. Edifying? Not exactly, but from their study Daniel and his friends emerged wiser than anyone else in the kingdom. They did so by reading, studying, and learning without *accepting* the many erroneous teachings of the Babylonians.

Similarly, as Milton discusses at some length in *Areopagitica*, the apostle Paul's marvelous speech before the Areopagus was littered with references to and quotations from secular Greek philosophers, including ones whose writings were largely antithetical to Christian thought. Paul had made a careful study of Athens, of its wisdom literature, of its monuments, statutes and idols, and of its culture, before he advanced before its body of sages to defend the gospel. Far from shunning, dismissing, or condemning secular wisdom, Paul engaged with it brilliantly and respectfully, refuting its errors and turning its admissions into arguments for the Christian faith.

Milton persuasively argues that, far from shying away from offending works, Christians should master them so as to be prepared to offer a defense of the faith. He points out that Christians familiar with anti-Christian literature would be the last thing the enemies of the faith would want. Milton notes that the Roman emperor, Julian the Apostate (the last pagan Roman emperor, who briefly succeeded the first Christian emperor, Constantine), "made a decree forbidding Christians the study of heathen learning; for, said he, they wound us with our own weapons, and with our own arts and sciences overcome us" (108). Conversely, the most successful anti-Christian writers make it their business to become intimately familiar with Scripture. With William Shakespeare, we can recognize from the account of Jesus' temptation in the wilderness that "the devil can cite Scripture for his purpose" (*The Merchant of Venice*, Act I, Scene 3). While we should probably not strive to know the devil's scriptures as well as he knows ours, Christians also should not adopt an attitude toward offending literature that leaves them less well-armed than their adversaries in the public arena.

BRING IT ON!

This book's thesis—that Christians should engage affirmatively, openly, and in good faith with works that challenge conventional Christian beliefs—is particularly important given the moment in the arc of Western civilization and American culture at which we find ourselves. Increasingly, norms of political correctness demand that speakers and writers refrain from saying anything that might offend the sensibilities of someone in the audience. We are called on to give "trigger warnings" if unpleasantness is to be discussed and to avoid "microaggressions," which can be anything that might offend a sensitive person. Slowly, but surely, society is creating a moral entitlement *not to be offended* by the speech of others.

This is bad news for everyone, and especially for Christians. The gospel cannot be presented without giving offense, for it is "a stumbling block to Jews and foolishness to Gentiles" (1 Cor. 1:23). The gospel must offend, because it shines a bright light on sin, insists that we are all hopelessly fallen and unable to recover through our own efforts, and demands repentance and belief in Jesus as the sole path to eternal life. An inoffensive gospel is no gospel at all.

Now, more than ever, Christians need to reject a censorial attitude with respect to offending books. If we demand censure of works that affront Christians—whether through the power of the state, other coercive means, or even just insult and invective, then what right should Christians have to boldly preach the gospel? Shouldn't our attitude be just the opposite? "Bring it on! (But then I get to say my piece, too)." That was Paul's attitude in the Areopagus, and it should be ours today.

In short, our attitude toward books that rock the church must embody the Golden Rule (Matt. 7:12). Do we want non-Christians to read the Bible with respect, open-mindedness, and diligence? If so, then how can the church promote censorship, *ad hominem* attacks, demonization, personal vilification, or unconsidered dismissal of books that offend Christians? What's good for the goose has to be good for the gander. As to offending books, as to all of life, Christians should lead the way in generosity of spirit, fairness, and humility.

And now, circling back to where we started; what, after all, does the church have to fear? That new works in science, philosophy, religion, psychology, mythology, economics, or politics will prove the Bible false? (In that case, we must have a rather weak faith in Scripture.) To quote Charles Spurgeon, the Christian isn't called on to defend Scripture any more than he's called on to defend a lion. Just open the cage door and let the lion out, and it will surely take care of itself. Or to paraphrase the wise Gamaliel (Acts 5), if a controversial book comes from human foolishness, then it will fail on its own; but if it speaks God's wisdom (even accidentally), then leveraging Scripture against it would be foolhardy indeed. To be sure, new books will come along and repeatedly rock the church, but we should welcome such moments as opportunities to deepen our faith and spread the gospel. The books we have studied here may have rocked the church, but our book—*The Book*—will rock the entire world.

Discussion Questions

CHAPTER 1: VALENTINUS

1. How would you define Gnosticism in your own words? Can you see its traces in popular culture today?

2. Was the church right to react with such hostility to *The Gospel of Truth* and other gnostic writings? What does it mean to call this work "heretical"? How did these teachings threaten the gospel message?

3. According to church historians, Valentinus came close to becoming the Bishop of Rome, or what today we would call the pope. What does that say about the development of Christian theology in the early church? About God's providence?

4. The early church fathers attacked not only the teachings of the gnostics but their personal reputations as well, accusing them of immorality and other sins. Are ad hominem attacks always out of place in theological arguments, or are they sometimes legitimate?

5. The text of *The Gospel of Truth* was lost to the world for a millennium and a half after the church banned the book. Then it was "miraculously" rediscovered, along with other gnostic texts. Why do you think God allowed for it to be rediscovered? Is this kind of question even worth asking?

6. What is a "forbidden fruit" effect? Is the church still creating forbidden fruit effects today?

7. In what ways does the contemporary church manifest gnostic beliefs or practices? Should any such tendencies be rooted out, accepted, or something in between?

CHAPTER 2: GALILEO

1. Why did the church feel so threatened by the Copernican system? Did its error come from a misreading of the Bible, or from something else?

2. The "Galileo Affair" had at least something to do with seventeenth-century battles between Catholics and Protestants. Can you think of any ways that disputes *among* Christians continue to have negative implications for science? //

3. Galileo argued that the Bible is supreme on "faith and morals," but that it has nothing to say about science. If we take Galileo's view, then there should never be a conflict between faith and science, since the Bible doesn't speak to scientific matters. Was Galileo right, or is his position too easy?

4. The "Galileo Affair" is often cited as evidence that the church is hostile to science. How would you answer that charge?

5. Are there any contemporary issues on which the church is allowing an overly rigid interpretation of Scripture or Christian tradition to get in the way of scientific inquiry? ?? good question

6. Some contemporary observers have argued that, even if Galileo's science was right, he should have introduced his discoveries with greater care because of the radical social implications they entailed. Do you agree that scientists should sometimes "soft-pedal" their discoveries in order to prevent harmful social or moral consequences?

7. How would you react to the announcement of an astonishing new scientific discovery that challenged your reading of the Bible—say, the existence of intelligent life on other planets? Would your first response be to deny the scientific discovery or reconsider your interpretation of the Bible? Does the Bible itself provide any instruction on how to react to new or threatening ideas?

CHAPTER 3: VOLTAIRE

1. *Candide* may have gone too far in mocking Christians and the church, but did it also raise any important criticisms that Christians should take to heart? Are any such criticisms still relevant to the church today?

2. How can Christians distinguish between the mockery of God and mockery of themselves? Is there a significant difference?

3. To be "Panglossian" is to take an overly optimistic view of the world, including that "everything will work out for the best." When terrible events happen—such as the Lisbon earthquake of 1755 or more recent catastrophes—how can Christians best assert the sovereignty and goodness of God without being or seeming insensitive to human suffering?

4. The church censored Voltaire, Voltaire advocated free speech, the French Revolution lionized Voltaire, and then the French Revolutionaries censored Christian works. What is the moral of this story?

5. Voltaire's moral character left much to be desired. Should his character be factored into an assessment of his ideas, or should his ideas be evaluated based solely on their own merits?

6. Many of the American founding fathers admired Voltaire for his wit, style, criticisms of the *Ancien Régime*, and advocacy for liberal reforms. Does that change your opinion of *Candide*?

7. When, if ever, is it appropriate for Christian authors to use satire or sarcasm? Should Christian literature be distinguished by a gentle and forthright tone that excludes satire, or is hard-hitting satire fair game also for Christian writers?

CHAPTER 4: DARWIN

1. Christians remain deeply divided over evolution today. Regardless of your views on the merits, do you agree that the church as a whole reacted badly to Darwin's theories? If so, then how could it have reacted better?

2. Chapter 4 identified three ways in which Darwin's theories challenged traditional Christian views on biblical interpretation, the nature of man, and the nature of God. Which of these, if any, do you find to be the most serious issue for Christian thought, and why?

3. During the Scopes Monkey Trial, fundamentalist Christianity was made to look ridiculous for opposing scientific progress. What lessons do you draw from the trial and its legacy for the church?

4. Darwin's theories have been taken to support some disturbing ideologies, from the eugenics movement, to social Darwinism, to Marxism. Is it fair to argue against Darwinism as a *scientific* theory based on its uses or misuses as a *social* or *political* ideology?

5. Contemporary atheists such as Richard Dawkins and Daniel Dennett argue that Darwinism is not just a scientific theory, but also a moral and philosophical theory that rebuts theism (and even deism). Should Christians respond by taking the position that evolution by natural selection is only a scientific theory with no moral or philosophical content (as Darwin himself argued), or should they embrace Dawkins's and Dennett's arguments as a further reason to dispute evolutionary theory?

6. The Galileo and Darwin affairs are often cited as connected dots in the church's "war against science." After reading chapters 2 and 4, are you convinced that these stories are similar, or are there important differences in the lessons for the church's interventions on scientific matters?

7. Whether or not you believe that Darwin's theories are fundamentally contrary to the Bible, what lessons do you draw from this story about how the church should prepare itself to confront the next big scientific theory challenging scriptural authority?

CHAPTER 5: MARX

1. Marx famously argued that "religion is the opium of the masses."
   What did he mean by that and was he right (keeping in mind
   that most Christians consider other world religions false)?

2. Why was Marx so hostile to Christianity? Is it possible for a
   Christian to support Marxism solely as an economic theory, or
   is Marxism necessarily more than that?

3. Marx argued that capitalism alienates men from their labor, and
   hence from themselves. The Bible teaches that men are alienated from God by sin. Do you experience feelings of alienation
   in your own life? If so, from what or whom do you feel alienated?
   Does comparing Marx to the biblical account of sin and separation from God help you make sense of your own experiences?

4. Many Christians respond to Marxism by asserting that poverty
   is the fault of the poor or simply a cross they should bear. Is the
   church itself partly to blame for the growth of Marxism? Does
   the Bible contain an economic message that answers Marxism?
   Is it dangerous to look for an economic message in the Bible?

5. In the book of Acts, we learn that the early church held property
   in common. Is the contemporary church too individualistic in
   its view of property, ownership, and wealth? If you believe that's
   true, does that mean Marx was on to something, or are we talk-
   ing about completely different questions?

6. Marx viewed history as a dialectic encounter between opposing
   material forces. What does that mean, and is it consistent or
   inconsistent with the biblical account of history?

7. Marxism failed miserably as a political and economic system
   in the Soviet Union and other Soviet bloc countries. What accounts for its continued allure to many people around the world
   two hundred years after the birth of Karl Marx?

CHAPTER 6: FREUD

1. Freud argued that religion is an illusion that man creates to give himself comfort against a violent and unjust world. Rather than rejecting Freud's argument out of hand, should Christians embrace it as an accurate description of religions other than Christianity?

2. Given Freud's emphasis on the subliminal and on early childhood development, it is tempting when reading about Freud's upbringing to turn his own theories back on him. Should Christians view Freud's biography—his experience as a secular (and somewhat anti-Semitic) Jew living in an increasingly troubled modern Europe and eventually falling under the thumb of the Nazis—in a different light?

3. It is easy to dismiss Freud based on some of the more bizarre or revolting aspects of his theories about sex. Has the church been too quick to throw out the baby with the bathwater as to Sigmund Freud?

4. Unlike many modern intellectuals, Freud took seriously the idea of original sin and guilt, to the point that he felt the need to invent a historical narrative—the original act of patricide (father murder)—to explain it. What can Christians take from Freud's argument that murderous rebellion against a father figure lies at the root of human guilt?

5. Speaking of fathers, Freud saw father-son relationships as pathologically complicated. Whatever your experiences with your own father, do Freud's theories provide any insight in understanding your relationship with God?

6. Some Christians see in Freud an uneasy ally against Enlightenment hyperrationalism, in particular in Freud's recognition of the subconscious and the conflicted nature of the human mind. Are there aspects of Freud's theories that you find helpful in defending a Christian worldview?

7. Oskar Pfister, the Swiss pastor, once wrote of Freud that "a powerful-minded opponent of religion is certainly of more service to it than a thousand useless supporters." Do you agree? If so, in what way was Freud of greatest service to the kingdom of God?

CHAPTER 7: CAMPBELL

1. Do you agree with Joseph Campbell that human folk stories and mythologies across time and place are part of a single, overarching "Monomyth" that share a common pattern, or do you agree more with his critics who say that Campbell exaggerated the commonality of the world's stories and mythologies?

2. Suppose it's true that many elements of the gospel story—for example, the virgin birth, the resurrection, and the ascension— are reflected in older stories from world mythology. From an analytical perspective, does that call into question the authenticity of the gospel account, strengthen the gospel's claims to truth, or have no effect either way?

3. C. S. Lewis and J. R. R. Tolkien—two important Christian writers of the twentieth century—believed that Christianity was "a true myth." Is that a contradiction in terms? What did they mean, and were they right?

4. What explains the tremendous impact that Campbell's theories have had on popular culture, such as the *Star Wars* movies? How should we speak to Christian young people about these influences? *Why Resurgence of movies, books, interests?*

5. Many Christians have seen Joseph Campbell as part of the "New Age" cult. What is the New Age, why should Christians worry about it, and was Campbell indeed part of it?

6. Joseph Campbell's most famous piece of advice was to "follow your bliss." Whatever Campbell may have meant by that, is "follow your bliss" a philosophy that Christians should embrace or reject?

7. The journalist Bill Moyers, who interviewed Campbell for the PBS *Power of Myth* series, asserted that Campbell liberated Moyers's Christian faith "from the cultural prisons to which it is sentenced." Whether or not you agree with Moyers regarding Campbell, do you agree that our faith can easily become entrapped in "cultural prisons"? Is reading books that challenge conventional Christian thinking a good way to break free from cultural prisons, even if much of the content of those books is erroneous? *yes!*

CHAPTER 8: THE NEXT SEVEN BOOKS

1. Looking back on the seven works surveyed in this book, can you identify any patterns in the church's response that should be reconsidered? What big lessons do you take away from the stories encountered in the first seven chapters?

2. Can you think of any books the church disapproves of today that might turn out to contain important truths? If so, what can you do about it?

3. John Milton argued that Christians can profit from reading materials even that are false. Was he right, or does a Christian have an obligation to seek the truth by reading works only by reliable authors?

4. Is it helpful to distinguish between censorship—that is, when a government or other authority suppresses a book—and disputing the substance of a book on its merits? Are there times when overly fierce condemnation of a book can turn into a kind of censorship?

5. The apostle Paul took advantage of the free speech tradition of the Athenian Areopagus to proclaim the gospel. Are you concerned that "political correctness" and animosity toward Christian points of view are diminishing Christians' ability to speak freely today? If so, are there any lessons or principles you can draw from the historical experience of Christians with books that rocked the church?

6. Has this book gone overboard in arguing that Christians should approach challenging books with an open, generous, and thoughtful mind? Aren't there books that really are dangerous to the church—dangerous even to read? How do we know when to be open-minded and when to "avoid godless chatter, because those who indulge in it will become more and more ungodly?" (2 Tim. 2:16).

7. All seven authors studied in this book received a Christian education and spent some time in the church, yet all seven went on to write books that posed serious challenges to conventional

Christian thinking. The future author of the next book that rocks the church may be in a Sunday school class, Christian school, or Christian home right now. Teachers, parents, other members of the Christian community, what have you learned from this book that might influence the way you interact with young people about difficult questions of faith and reason?

Notes

CHAPTER 1

1. This account of the discovery of the Nag Hammadi scrolls is based on Elaine Pagels, *The Gnostic Gospels* (New York: Random House, 1979), and J. M. Robinson, introduction to *The Nag Hammadi Library* (New York: Harper & Row, 1977).

2. Robinson, 22.

3. Throughout this book, I use the word *orthodox* without capitalization to refer to the mainstream of the Christian tradition, as comprehending the Roman Catholic, Eastern Orthodox, and Protestant wings. When I mean to refer to the Eastern Orthodox tradition specifically, I denote my meaning by capitalizing "Orthodox."

4. *The Gospel of Thomas*, in *The Nag Hammadi Scriptures: The Revised and Updated Translation of Sacred Gnostic Texts*, ed. Marvin Meyer (New York: HarperOne, 2007).

5. The term "pope" did not come into usage until the third century AD, after the time of Valentinus, so in his time he would have been known as "Bishop of Rome." The office he held, however, was what the church would later recognize as a papacy extending back to Simon Peter.

6. The biographic sketch that follows is drawn largely from the following sources: G. S. R. Mead, *Fragments of a Faith Forgotten* (1906); *The Oxford Dictionary of the Christian Church*, 2nd ed. (Oxford: Oxford University Press, 1974); Peter Lampe, *From Paul to Valentinus: Christians at Rome in the First Two Centuries*, trans. Michael Steinhauser (Minneapolis, MN: Fortress Press, 2003).

7. Mead, 294.

8. Hippolytus of Rome, *Philosophumena* (London: Aeterna Press, 2015), 137.

9. Quintus Tertullian, *Against the Valentinians* (Savage, MN: Lighthouse Publishing, 2015).

10. Francis Legge, *Forerunners and Rivals of Christianity: From 330 B.C. to 330 A.D.*, vol. 1 (New Hyde Park, NY: University Books, 1964), 118.

11. Mead, 296.

12. Legge, 118.

13. Mead, 147.

14. Irenaeus, *Against Heresies* (Pickerington, OH: Beloved, 2015), 3.11.19.

15. Henry Chadwick, *The Early Church*, rev. ed. (New York: Penguin Putnam, 1993), 37.

16. A few scholars do not consider the *Gospel of Truth* to be fully gnostic insofar as it seems to endorse the fact of a physical incarnation.

17. *Gospel of Truth*, in *The Nag Hammadi Scriptures: The Revised and Updated Translation of Sacred Gnostic Texts*, ed. Marvin Meyer (New York: HarperOne, 2007), 36. For the rest of this chapter, citations for *Gospel of Truth* will be indicated in parentheses in the text.

18. Mead, 308.

19. Tertullian, *Against All Heresies*, bk. 1, ch. 4.

20. Irenaeus, 235.

21. Tertullian, bk. 1, ch. 4.

22. Hippolytus, 135.

23. See, for example, Chadwick, 40.

24. Pagels, 6.

25. Pagels, 13–14.

26. Pagels, 134.

27. Pagels, 97.

28. Irenaeus, 19.

29. Ramsay MacMullen, *Christianizing the Roman Empire: A.D. 100–400* (New Haven, CT: Yale University Press, 1984), 101.

30. Bart D. Ehrman, *Lost Christianities: The Battles for Scripture and the Faiths We Never Knew* (Oxford: Oxford University Press, 2003), 129.

31. Kurt Rudolph, *Gnosis*, trans. Robert McLachlan Wilson (San Francisco: Harper & Row, 1983), 12.

32. Alfred von Harnack, *History of Dogma* (New York: Dover, 1961), 228.

33. Mead, 145.

34. Harold Bloom, *The American Religion: The Emergence of the Post-Christian Nation* (New York: Simon & Schuster, 1992), 30.

CHAPTER 2

1. J. L. Heilbron, *Galileo* (Oxford: Oxford University Press, 2010), 317.

2. Heilbron, 148.

3. Galileo Galilei, *The Starry Messenger*, in *The Essential Galileo*, ed. and trans. Maurice A. Finocchiaro (Indianapolis, IN: Hackett, 2008), 45–46. For the rest of this chapter, citations for *The Starry Messenger* will be indicated in parentheses in the text by *SM* and the page number.

4. Galileo Galilei, *Dialogue on the Two Chief World Systems*, in *The Essential Galileo*, ed. and trans. Maurice A. Finocchiaro (Indianapolis, IN: Hackett, 2008), 190. For the rest of this chapter, citations for the *Dialogue* will be indicated in parentheses in the text by *D* and the page number.

5. Heilbron, 213.

6. "Inquisition's Sentence" (22 June 1633), in *The Essential Galileo*, ed. and trans. Maurice A. Finocchiaro (Indianapolis, IN: Hackett, 2008), 289.

7. "Inquisition's Sentence," 289.

8. Joseph Ratzinger, *Turning Point for Europe? The Church in the Modern World—Assessment and Forecast*, trans. Brian McNeil from the 1991 German ed. (San Francisco: Ignatius Press, 1994).

9. Stephen Hawking, *A Brief History of Time: From the Big Bang to Black Holes* (New York: Bantam, 1988), 116.

10. Andrew D. White, *A History of the Warfare of Science with Theology in Christendom* (New York: Appleton 1896), 126.

11. Thomas S. Kuhn, *The Copernican Revolution* (Cambridge, MA: Harvard University Press, 1957), ch. 6.

12. Kuhn, 195.

13. Kuhn, 196.

14. Owen Gingerich, "Did the Reformers Reject Copernicus?" in *Christianity Today* 76 (2002).

CHAPTER 3

1. Ian Davidson, *Voltaire: A Life* (New York: Pegasus Books, 2010), 461.

2. Davidson, 88.

3. Voltaire, *A Treatise on Toleration and Other Essays*, trans. Joseph McCabe (Amherst, NY: Prometheus Books, 1994), 1, 5.

4. Davidson, 460.

5. Davidson, 183.

6. Voltaire, *Epitres*, XCVI (1770).

7. Voltaire, *Candide* (Mineola, NY: Dover, 1991), 9. For the rest of this chapter, citations for *Candide* will be indicated in parentheses in the text.

8. Will Durant, *The Story of Civilization Volume 9: The Age of Voltaire* (New York: Simon & Schuster, 1965), 724.

9. Haydn Mason, *Candide: Optimism Demolished* (New York: Twayne, 1992).

10. Ian Davidson, *Voltaire in Exile* (New York: Grove Press, 2004), 53–54.

11. Mason, 14.

12. Paul S. Boyer, *Purity in Print: Book Censorship in America from the Gilded Age to the Computer Age* (Madison: University of Wisconsin Press, 2002), 209.

13. Saul D. Alinsky, *Rules for Radicals: A Pragmatic Primer for Realistic Radicals* (New York: Vintage Books, 1971).

14. Aldous Huxley, *On the Margin* (New York: Doran, 1923), 21-22.

15. C. S. Lewis, *The Problem of Pain* (1940; repr., New York: HarperOne, 2015).

16. Voltaire, "A Treatise on Toleration," in *A Treatise on Toleration and Other Essays*, trans. Joseph McCabe (Amherst, NY: Prometheus Books, 1994), 187.

17. Fernando Báez, *A Universal History of the Destruction of Books: From Ancient Sumer to Modern Iraq*, trans. Alfred MacAdam (New York: Atlas & Co, 2004), 160.

18. Báez, 161.

CHAPTER 4

1. Edward J. Larson, *Evolution: The Remarkable History of a Scientific Theory* (New York: The Modern Library, 2004), 201.

2. Randy Moore and William F. McComas, *The Scopes Monkey Trial* (Charleston, SC: Arcadia, 2016), 63.

3. Moore and McComas, 83.

4. H. L. Mencken, *A Religious Orgy in Tennessee* (Hoboken, NJ: Melville House, 1925), 108.

5. Charles Darwin, *The Autobiography of Charles Darwin*, ed. Nora Barlow (New York: Harcourt, Brace, 1958), 72.

6. Larson, 67.

7. Janet Browne, *Charles Darwin Voyaging* (Princeton, NJ: Princeton University Press, 1995), 296.

8. Charles Darwin, *Foundations of the Origin of Species: Two Essays Written in 1842 and 1844*, ed. Francis Darwin (Cambridge: Cambridge University Press, 1909), 182.

9. Larson, 70.

10. Charles Darwin, *The Origin of Species By Means of Natural Selection or the Preservation of Favoured Races in the Struggle for Life* (New York: Penguin Group, 1958), 31. For the rest of this chapter, citations for *The Origin of Species* will be indicated in parentheses in the text.

11. Larson, 80.

12. Janet Browne, *Charles Darwin: The Power of Place* (Princeton, NJ: Princeton University Press, 2002), 403.

13. Charles Hodge, *What Is Darwinism?* (New York: Scribner, 1974), 11, 173.

14. J. R. Lucas, *Wilberforce and Huxley: A Legendary Encounter*, http://users.ox.ac.uk/~jrlucas/legend.html.

15. Moore and McComas, 16.

16. Moore and McComas, 16.

17. Moore and McComas, 16.

18. Billy Graham, *Billy Graham: Personal Thoughts of a Public Man* (Colorado Springs: Chariot Victor, 1997), 72–74.

19. Daniel C. Dennett, *Darwin's Dangerous Idea: Evolution and the Meaning of Life* (New York: Simon & Schuster, 1995), 18.

20. Mark A. Noll, *The Scandal of the Evangelical Mind* (Grand Rapids: Eerdmans, 1994), 197.

CHAPTER 5

1. John Noble Wilford, "James B. Irwin, 61, Ex-Astronaut; Founded Religious Organization," *New York Times*, August 10, 1991.

2. Robert Payne, *Marx* (London: Simon & Schuster, 1968), 20.

3. David McClellan, *Karl Marx: A Biography* (New York: MacMillan, 2006), 9.

4. Karl Marx, *Karl Marx: Early Writings*, trans. T. B. Bottomore (New York: McGraw Hill, 1963).

5. Paul Johnson, *Intellectuals* (New York: Harper & Rowe, 1988), 73.

6. Karl Marx, *Critique of Hegel's Philosophy of Right* (1843), trans. Joseph O'Malley (Cambridge: Cambridge University Press, 1977).

7. Payne, 251.

8. Payne, 251.

9. Johnson, 80.

10. Johnson, 82. Johnson notes that Freddy "died in January 1929, by which time Marx's vision of the dictatorship of the proletariat had taken concrete and terrifying shape, and Stalin—the ruler who achieved the absolute power for which Marx had yearned—was just beginning his catastrophic assault on the Russian peasantry."

11. Frederick Engels, *Preface to The Communist Manifesto*, authorized English translation (1888; repr., New York: International Publishers, 1948).

12. Karl Marx and Frederick Engels, *The Communist Manifesto*, authorized English translation 1888 (New York: International Publishers, 1948), 8. For the rest of this chapter, citations for *The Communist Manifesto* will be indicated in parentheses in the text.

13. McLellan, 397.

14. Karl Marx, *National Economy and Philosophy* (1844).

15. Karl Marx, *The German Ideology* (1846).

16. John Piper, *Five Cheers for the Church and Individualism*, August 13, 2013, http://www.desiringgod.org/articles/five-cheers-for-the-church-and-individualism.

17. C. S. Lewis, *Mere Christianity* (New York: HarperOne, 1980), 185.

18. Denis R. Janz, *World Christianity and Marxism* (Oxford: Oxford University Press, 1998), 17.

19. Janz, 17.

20. Janz, 17.

21. Janz, 19.

22. William Temple, *The Kingdom of God* (1912); qtd. in Janz, 27.

23. George M. Marsden, *Fundamentalism and American Culture* (Oxford: Oxford University Press, 2006), 209.

24. Marsden, 209.

25. Marsden, 209.

26. Marsden, 209.

27. Mark A, Noll, *A History of Christianity in the United States and Canada* (Grand Rapids: Eerdmans, 1992), 440.

28. Janz, 23.

29. Janz, 23.

30. Janz, 63.

31. Catholic News Agency, "Former Soviet Spy: We Created Liberation Theology," http://www.catholicnewsagency.com/news/former-soviet-spy-we -created-liberation-theology-83634/.

32. Janz, 83–96.

33. Vladimir Lenin, *Selected Works* (1939).

34. Louis Menand, "Karl Marx, Yesterday and Today," *The New Yorker*, October 10, 2016.

35. From http://victimsofcommunism.org/new-report-reveals-u-s-atti tudes-on-socialism-communism-on-eve-of-2016-election/.

36. Karl Marx, *Das Capital:* "The religious reflex of the real world can . . . only vanish, when the practical relations of every-day life offer to man none but perfectly intelligible and reasonable relations with regard to his fellow man and to nature."

CHAPTER 6

1. Lewis Cohen, "How Sigmund Freud Wanted to Die," *The Atlantic*, September 23, 2014.

2. Peter Gay, *Freud: A Life for Our Time* (New York: W. W. Norton, 1998), 592–93.

3. Sigmund Freud, *The Future of an Illusion* (Peterborough, ON: Broadview Press, 2012), 87–88. For the rest of this chapter, citations for *The Future of an Illusion* will be indicated in parentheses in the text.

4. Todd Dufresne, Introduction, *Sigmund Freud: The Future of an Illusion* (Peterborough, ON: Broadview Press, 2012), 11.

5. Maryse Choisy, *Sigmund Freud: A New Appraisal* (New York: Philosophical Library, 1963), 84.

6. Gay, 535–36.

7. Oskar Pfister, "The Illusion of a Future: A Friendly Dispute with Professor Sigmund Freud (1928)," in *Sigmund Freud: The Future of an Illusion* (Peterborough, ON: Broadview Press, 2012), 122.

8. Pfister, 116.

9. Gay, 537.

10. Gay, 537.

11. Gay, 646.

12. Sigmund Freud, *An Autobiographical Study* (New York: W. W. Norton, 1935), 102–3.

13. Douglas Carl Adams, *Old-Time Religion Embracing Modernist Culture: American Fundamentalism between the Wars* (Lanham, MD: Lexington Books, 2016), 62.

14. Adams, 62.

15. William R. Newell, *Romans Verse-by-Verse* (Grand Rapids: Christian Classics Ethereal Library, 1938).

16. Adams, 58.

17. C. S. Lewis, *Mere Christianity* (New York: HarperOne, 1952), 89.

18. John M. Perry, *Tillich's Response to Freud: A Christian Answer to the Freudian Critique of Religion* (New York: University Press of America, 1988), ix (italics original).

19. Reinhold Niebuhr, "Human Creativity and Self-Concern in Freud's Thought," in *Freud and the 20th Century*, ed. Benjamin Nelson (New York: Meridian Books, 1957).

20. Niebuhr, 260.

21. Niebuhr, 269.

22. Albert Mohler, "The Seduction of Pornography and the Integrity of Christian Marriage," May 29, 2012, http://www.albertmohler.com/2012/05/29/the-seduction-of-pornography-and-the-integrity-of-christian-marriage-part-one-2/.

23. Steven Pinker, *How the Mind Works* (New York: W. W. Norton, 1997), 460.

24. Frederick Crews, "The Verdict on Freud," *Psychological Science* (March 1996).

25. R. Atkinson, R. C. Atkinson, E. E. Smith, D. J. Bem, and S. Nolen-Hoeksema, eds., *Hilgard's Introduction to Psychology*, 13th ed. (New York: Harcourt Brace Jovanovich, 2000).

26. Maureen Dowd, "Oedipus Rex Complex," *New York Times*, January 3, 2012.

Chapter 7

1. Joseph Campbell with Bill Moyers, *The Power of Myth* (New York: Doubleday, 1988), 56–57. For the rest of this chapter, citations for *The Power of Myth* will be indicated as *PM* with page number in parentheses in the text.

2. Stephen Larsen and Robin Larsen, *Joseph Campbell: A Fire in the Mind* (New York: Doubleday, 2002), 3.

3. See https://www.jcf.org/about-joseph-campbell.

4. Andrea Chambers and Maria Speidel, "Bill Moyers Angrily Defends Joseph Campbell against Charges That His Wisdom Was Only a Myth," *People* (November 27, 1989).

5. Joseph Campbell, *The Hero with a Thousand Faces*, 3d ed. (Novato, CA: New York Library, 2008), xii. For the rest of this chapter, citations for *The*

Hero with a Thousand Faces will be indicated by *HTF* and page number in parentheses in the text.

6. Lord Raglan, *The Hero: A Study in Tradition, Myth and Drama by Lord Raglan* (Mineola, NY: Dover, 1936).

7. Francis Lee Utley, "Lincoln Wasn't There, or Lord Raglan's Hero," *CEA Chap Book* (Washington, DC: College English Association, 1965); supplement to *The CEA Critic* 22 (June 1965).

8. C. S. Lewis, "Myth Became Fact," *God in the Dock* (Grand Rapids: Eerdmans, 1970), 58.

9. J. R. R. Tolkien, "On Fairy Stories," *The Monsters and the Critics and Other Essays*, ed. Christopher Tolkien (London: HarperCollins, 2006), 109–61.

10. See *The Joseph Campbell Phenomenon: Implications for the Contemporary Church*, ed. Lawrence Madden (Washington, DC: The Pastoral Press, 1992); and *Paths to the Power of Myth: Joseph Campbell and the Study of Religion*, ed. Daniel C. Noel (New York: The Crossroad, 1990).

11. Brian O. McDermott, "The Campbell Phenomenon and the Uniqueness of Jesus Christ," *The Joseph Campbell Phenomenon: Implications for the Contemporary Church*, ed. Lawrence Madden (Washington, DC: The Pastoral Press, 1992).

12. McDermott, 99.

13. McDermott, 92.

14. Mortimer J. Adler, "This Campbell Person," in *National Review* (February 17, 1992): 49.

15. Elliot Miller, *A Crash Course on the New Age Movement: Describing and Evaluating a Growing Social Force* (Grand Rapids: Baker, 1989), 185.

16. Douglas Groothius, *Christian History Sampler: History Behind the News*, Issue 26 (1990).

17. A personal note: Despite the claim I just made in the text, I first encountered Joseph Campbell through the sympathetic lens of Father Joseph McClatchey in a course on modern mythology at Wheaton College in the early 1990s.

18. Tom Snyder, *Myth Conceptions: Joseph Campbell and the New Age* (Grand Rapids: Baker, 1995).

19. Snyder, 19.

20. Snyder, 81.

21. Snyder, 52.

22. Snyder, 52.

23. Larsen and Larsen, 414.

24. Belden C. Lane, "The Power of Myth: Lessons from Joseph Campbell," *The Christian Century* (July1989), 652.

25. "Joseph Campbell: An Exchange," *New York Review of Books*, November 9, 1989, 57.

26. Alan Dundes, "Folkloristics in the Twenty-First Century," *J. Am. Folklore* 118, no. 470 (2005): 385–408.

27. See, for example, Richard G. Howe and Norman L. Geisler, *The Religion of the Force*, 2nd ed. (Matthews, NC: Bastion Books, 2015).

28. Bob and Gretchen Passantino, foreword to Tom Snyder, *Myth Conceptions: Joseph Campbell and the New Age* (Grand Rapids: Baker, 1995).

CHAPTER 8

1. John Milton, *Areopagitica*, in John Milton, *Areopagitica and Other Writings*, ed. William Poole (New York: Penguin, 2014), 101. For the rest of this chapter, citations for *Areopagitica* will be indicated in parentheses in the text.

2. The first printed version of *Areopagitica* uses the word "wayfaring" here, but Milton appears to have changed it to "warfaring" in subsequent versions. *Areopagitica*, ed. notes, 326n53.

Selected Bibliography

PRIMARY SOURCES

Campbell, Joseph. *The Hero with a Thousand Faces*. 3d ed. Novato, CA: New York Library, 2008.

Campbell, Joseph, with Bill Moyers. *The Power of Myth*. New York: Doubleday, 1988.

Darwin, Charles. *The Autobiography of Charles Darwin*. Edited by Nora Barlow. New York: Harcourt, Brace, 1958.

———. *The Descent of Man*. New York: Penguin Books, 2004.

———. *The Origin of Species by Means of Natural Selection or the Preservation of Favoured Races in the Struggle for Life*. New York: The Penguin Group, 1958.

———. *Voyage of the Beagle*. New York: Penguin Books, 1989.

Freud, Sigmund. *Beyond the Pleasure Principle*. New York, W.W. Norton, 1990

———. *Civilization and its Discontents*. New York: W. W. Norton, 1989.

———. *The Ego and the Id*. New York: W. W. Norton, 1990.

———. *The Future of an Illusion*. Buffalo, NY: Broadview Editions, 2012.

———. *Moses and Monotheism*. New York: Vintage Press, 1955.

———. *The Question of Lay Analysis*. New York: W. W. Norton, 1978.

———. *Totem and Taboo*. New York: W. W. Norton, 1990.

Galilei, Galileo. *Discoveries and Opinions of Galileo*. Translated by Stillman Drake. New York: Anchor Books, 1957.

———. *The Essential Galileo*. Translated by Maurice A. Finocchiaro. Indianapolis: Hackett, 2008.

Marx, Karl. *Capital, Vol 1*. Translated by Ben Fowkes. New York: Penguin Classics, 1992.

———. *Critique of Hegel's Philosophy of Right*. Cambridge: Cambridge University Press, 1977.

Marx, Karl, and Frederick Engels. *The Communist Manifesto.* New York: International Publishers, 1948. From the authorized English translation 1888.

Milton, John. *Areopagitica and Other Writings.* New York: Penguin Classics, 2014.

Valentinus. *The Gospel of Truth.* In *The Nag Hammadi Scriptures: The Revised and Updated Translation of Sacred Gnostic Texts.* Edited by Marvin Meyer. New York: HarperOne, 2007.

Voltaire. *Candide.* Mineola, NY: Dover Thrift, 1991.

———. *A Treatise on Toleration and Other Essays.* Translated by Joseph McCabe. Amherst, NY: Prometheus Books, 1994.

Secondary Sources

Báez, Fernando. *A Universal History of the Destruction of Books from Ancient Sumer to Modern Iraq.* Translated by Alfred MacAdam. New York: Atlas & Co., 2008.

Blazer, Dan. *Freud vs. God: How Psychiatry Lost Its Soul & Christianity Lost Its Mind.* Downers Grove, IL: InterVarsity Press, 1998.

Bloom, Harold. *The American Religion: The Emergence of the Post-Christian Nation.* New York: Simon & Schuster, 1992.

Browne, Janet. *Charles Darwin: The Power of Place.* Princeton: Princeton University Press, 2002.

———. *Charles Darwin Voyaging.* Princeton: Princeton University Press, 1995.

Chadwick, Henry. *The Early Church: The Story of Emergent Christianity from the Apostolic Age to the Dividing of the Ways between the Greek East and Latin West.* Rev. ed. New York: Penguin Books, 1993.

Davidson, Ian. *Voltaire: A Life.* New York: Pegasus Books, 2010.

———. *Voltaire in Exile: The Last Years, 1753–78.* New York: Grove Press, 2004.

Dawkins, Richard. *The God Delusion.* New York: Mariner Books, 2008.

Dennett, Daniel C. *Darwin's Dangerous Idea: Evolution and the Meaning of Life.* New York: Simon & Schuster, 1995.

Ehrman, Bart D. *Lost Christianities: The Battles for Scripture and the Faiths We Never Knew.* Oxford: Oxford University Press, 2003.

Gay, Peter. *Freud: A Life for Our Time.* 3d. ed. New York: W. W. Norton, 2006.

Heilbron, J. L. *Galileo.* Oxford: Oxford University Press, 2010.

Hippolytus of Rome. *Philosophumena.* London: Aeterna Press, 2015.

Howe, Richard G., and Norman L. Geisler. 2nd ed. *The Religion of the Force.* Matthews, NC: Bastion Books, 2015.

Irenaeus. *Against Heresies.* London: Aeterna Press, 2016.

Janz, Dennis R. *World Christianity and Marxism.* Oxford: Oxford University Press, 1998.

Johnson, Paul. *Intellectuals.* New York: Harper & Rowe, 1988.

Johnson, Phillip E. *Darwin on Trial.* 3d ed. Downers Grove, IL: IVP Books, 2010.

Lampe, Peter. *From Paul to Valentinus: Christians at Rome in the First Two Centuries.* Minneapolis, MN: Fortress Press, 2003.

Larsen, Stephen, and Robin Larsen. *Joseph Campbell: A Fire in the Mind.* New York: Doubleday, 2002.

Larson, Edward J. *Evolution: The Remarkable History of a Scientific Theory.* New York: The Modern Library, 2004.

———. *Summer for the Gods: The Scopes Trial and America's Continuing Debate Over Science and Religion.* New York: Perseus Books, 1997.

Legge, Francis. *Forerunners and Rivals of Christianity: From 330 B.C. to 330 A.D.* New Hyde Park, NY: University Books, 1964.

Lewis, C. S. *Essay Collection: Faith, Christianity and the Church.* New York: HarperCollins, 2000.

———. *God in the Dock: Essays on Theology and Ethics.* Grand Rapids, MI: Eerdmans, 2014.

———. *Mere Christianity.* New York: HarperOne, 1980.

MacIntyre, Alasdair. *Marxism and Christianity.* South Bend, IN: University of Notre Dame Press, 1984.

MacMullen, Ramsay. *Christianizing the Roman Empire: A.D. 100–400.* New Haven, CT: Yale University Press, 1984.

Madden, Lawrence, ed. *The Joseph Campbell Phenomenon: Implications for the Contemporary Church.* Washington: The Pastoral Press, 1992.

Marsden, George M. *Fundamentalism and American Culture.* 2nd ed. Oxford: Oxford University Press, 2006.

Mason, Haydn. *Candide: Optimism Demolished.* New York: Twayne Publishers, 1992.

McLellan, David. *Karl Marx: A Biography*. 4th ed. New York: Palgrave Macmillan, 2006.

Mead, G. R. S. *Fragments of a Faith Forgotten*. Lyndhurst, NJ: Mystical World Reprints, 2012.

Mencken, H. L. *A Religious Orgy in Tennessee: A Reporter's Account of the Scopes Monkey Trial*. Hokboken, NJ: Melville House, 2006.

Menzies, James W. *True Myth: C. S. Lewis and Joseph Campbell on the Veracity of Christianity*. Eugene, OR: Pickwick Publications, 2014.

Meyer, Marvin, ed. *The Nag Hammadi Scriptures*. New York: Harper-One, 2007.

Moore, Randy, and William F. McComas. *The Scopes Monkey Trial*. Charleston, SC: Arcadia Publishing, 2016.

Moran, Jeffrey P. *The Scopes Trial: A Brief History with Documents*. Boston: Bedford / St. Martin's, 2002.

Nelsen, Benjamin, ed. *Freud and the 20th Century*. New York: Meridian Books, 1957.

Nicholi, Armand M., Jr. *C. S. Lewis and Sigmund Freud Debate God, Love, Sex, and the Meaning of Life*. New York: The Free Press, 2002.

Noel, Daniel C., ed. *Paths to the Power of Myth: Joseph Campbell and the Study of Religion*. New York: Crossroad, 1990.

Noll, Mark A. *The Scandal of the Evangelical Mind*. Grand Rapids, MI: Eerdmans, 1994.

Pagels, Elaine. *The Gnostic Gospels*. New York: Vintage Books, 1989.

Payne, Robert. *Marx: A Biography*. New York: Simon & Schuster, 1968.

Perry, John M. *Tillich's Response to Freud: A Christian Answer to the Freudian Critique of Religion*. Lanham, MD: University Press of America, 1988.

Plantinga, Alvin. *Where the Conflict Really Lies: Science, Religion, & Naturalism*. Oxford: Oxford University Press, 2011.

Rudolph, Kurt. *Gnosis: The Nature and History of Gnosticism*. Translated by Robert McLachlan. New York: Harper & Rowe, 1983.

Snyder, Tom. *Myth Conceptions: Joseph Campbell and the New Age*. Grand Rapids, MI: Baker, 1995.

Weiner, Jonathan. *The Beak of the Finch*. New York: Vintage Books, 1994.

White, Andrew D. *A History of the Warfare of Science with Theology in Christendom*. Buffalo, NY: Prometheus Books, 1993.